FROM DNA TO DEAN

AMONG BOOKS BY THE SAME AUTHOR:

Science and the Christian Experiment (OUP, Oxford 1971)

Creation and the World of Science, 1978 Bampton Lectures (Clarendon Press, Oxford 1979)

God's Creation and the World of Science, 1981 Bishop Williams Memorial Lectures; Translated into Japanese by D. O. Tsukada and M. Seki (Shinkyo Shuppansha, 1983)

The Physical Chemistry of Biological Organization (Clarendon Press, Oxford 1983)

Intimations of Reality – Critical Realism in Science and Religion, 1983 Meldenhall Lectures (University of Notre Dame Press, 1984)

God and the New Biology (Dent, 1986; reprinted Peter Smith, Gloucester, Mass., 1994)

Theology for a Scientific Age: Being and Becoming – Natural, Divine and Human (SCM Press, 1993) Enlarged paperback of earlier edition (Blackwell, 1990) incorporating additionally the 1993 Gifford Lectures at St Andrews University.

From DNA to DEAN

Reflections and Explorations of a Priest-Scientist

by

ARTHUR PEACOCKE

The Canterbury Press
Norwich

© Arthur Peacocke 1996
First published 1996 by The Canterbury Press Norwich
(a publishing imprint of Hymns Ancient & Modern Limited,
a registered charity)
St Mary's Works, St Mary's Plain,
Norwich, Norfolk, NR3 3BH

British Library Cataloguing in Publication Data

A catalogue record for this book is available
from the British Library

ISBN 1-85311-132-5

*Typeset by David Gregson Associates and
Printed and bound in Great Britain by
St Edmundsbury Press Limited
Bury St Edmunds, Suffolk*

To the members of

Clare College, Cambridge,
and
Exeter College, Oxford,

in whose Chapels as Dean and Catechist,
respectively,

I was stimulated to formulate many of these reflections.

CONTENTS

PREFACE

Any scientist, especially if connected with biology, who professes any attachment to the Christian faith is liable to encounter incredulity on the part of many acquaintances whose received mythology is that of 'the warfare of science and religion'. Although this mythology is well-entrenched in the media, the fact is that, in recent decades and in spite of this cultural pressure, many of those engaged in the scientific enterprise have been able with intellectual integrity to follow the Christian 'Way' (as it was called in the early days of the church). Amongst these I include myself. The path is not always smooth from scepticism and agnosticism to faith for continuously new challenges arise from the changing perspectives on the world of the ever-expanding horizons of scientific inquiry. This is as it should be, for any synthesis of perceptions of God, humanity and nature must integrate, or at least be consonant with, the knowledge of humanity and nature that the sciences provide – as well as with new theological insights. So any scientist who espouses the Christian faith in any of its variegated forms must be perennially engaged in a continuous dialogue between his or her science and faith.

In my case, as the autobiographical Part I of this volume outlines, this dialogue led me from agnosticism to active participation in the life of the Church (of England, in my case) and eventually to ordination within it as 'worker-priest', more precisely a 'priest-scientist'. As it happened, ordination in 1971 divides my adult life into roughly equal periods since graduation, spent entirely at universities: some 27 years as a full-time research and teaching physical biochemist; and 25 years as a priest, during which my scientific work did not come to an end. This therefore seemed an appropriate point at which to collect together some of the fruits of my reflections that have appeared not in books but in articles and in unpublished addresses given in the contexts of college and university life.

These shorter pieces, which constitute Part II, focus on themes
in Christian faith and practice. They inevitably bear the imprint of
my formation (*Bildung*) as a scientist. This irrevocably stamps
one with the urge to ask 'Why?' and 'What is the evidence for?'
in all matters, not least those concerning Christian belief. I hope
they will be helpful to those seeking a faith with intellectual
integrity. For I have found that the disjunction experienced in
relation to the already-mentioned incredulity of those, especially
scientists, when confronted with the existence of a *priest*-scien-
tist, is matched by the incomprehension of traditionally trained
clergy who have no perception whatever of the challenge of the
scientific worldview to received Christian belief. They just
cannot understand where many of us priest-scientists are 'coming
from' in our theological questionings which, to them, seem tinged
with unwarranted scepticism. We continue to go on asking the
'Why' questions imprinted in our approach to all phenomena,
both natural and 'religious'.

I have therefore concluded this volume with three expositions
(Part III) which pull together in a more systematic way many of
the themes scattered throughout the reflections of Part II. The first
(chap. 24) outlines briefly how I conceive of the relation of the
'old' theological traditions to 'new' knowledge. The second
(chap. 25) faces up to the challenge to the thought and beliefs of
the Church from what we now know from the sciences about
humanity and the world and their history. The third (chap. 26)
gives a fuller account than elsewhere in this volume, at least, of
the basis of my religion as a natural scientist and how it has
developed. In this last and longest chapter I unashamedly echo
the concerns and intentions of the incomparable Sir Thomas
Browne in that ever-fresh work of his from the seventeenth-
century – his *Religio Medici* (*The Religion of a Physician*). If I
have been able to persuade one contemporary scientifically-
cultured despiser of the Christian faith to take its intellectual
content and thrust seriously as effectively as he did, I shall be well
content.

The double-stranded course of my life as a priest-scientist
has been less rosy and comfortable professionally than the
outsider's image of universities as ivory towers would depict.

Many decisions have been difficult and some led to dead ends. I have only been able to pursue my double vocation through the understanding and unswerving support of my wife, Rosemary, whose direct, unflinching and cheerful faith has provided a rock in the storms. More immediately, I am also indebted to her for her help in editing the sometimes wayward texts of these variegated contributions – I am for this, and innumerable other unspoken reasons, glad to have this opportunity of here expressing my gratitude in print.

Acknowledgements

I am grateful to The Crossroad Publishing Company, New York, for permission to reproduce, with only minor modifications, 'From DNA to DEAN' from *Reasoned Faith: Essays on the Interplay of Faith and Reason*, a Tulane Judeo-Christian Studies Edition, edited by Frank Birtel, Copyright © 1993 by the Chair of Judeo-Christian Studies, Tulane University. All rights reserved. I am also grateful to the editors of *Zygon* for permission to reproduce this same chapter 1 and chapter 26 published, respectively, in issues 26 (1991) 477–493, and 29 (1994) 639–659; and to the editor of *Modern Believing* for permission to publish as chapter 25 a longer version of an article of the same title which appeared in the issue of October, XXXVI, No. 4 (1995) 15–26 (originally given as a lecture on 26th September, 1994, to members of the Faith and Science Exchange at Boston University School of Theology, USA and to the Oxford Diocesan Conference on 22nd March, 1995).

PART I

AUTOBIOGRAPHICAL

1

From DNA to DEAN

Since we all start life as strands of the genetical material DNA, a percipient reader of the title of this book might surmise that the letter E added to DNA in the title's final word could stand for 'everything else' *Everything* else? Are we nothing but DNA? Or, to put it another way – Are we nothing but DNA's way of making more DNA? Or, are we, on the other hand, *persons* – centres of self-consciousness communicating by words and symbols our thoughts and feelings and intuitions, all of which are as real as DNA? Such questions cannot but dog the pathway of any trained and sensitive scientist concerned with the human condition. In my case, the attempt to respond to them has shaped not only my thinking but also my path through life.

First, then there is about us all what we might call 'the DNA story' – the account of our origins, where we came from and what we have inherited biologically, personally and culturally.

I was young enough at the outbreak of war in 1939, and still young enough in 1942, not to be called up into the armed forces. So, from a semi-suburban, semi-industrial, semi-rural town, some twenty miles northwest of London, then still on the edge of fine open English countryside, I went 'up' to Oxford with a scholarship in natural science to 'read' chemistry. My interest in the subject had been roused mainly through some first-class teaching I had received at my local grammar school (in Watford, Hertfordshire) where I had a non-fee-paying scholarship place. My home was not at all bookish – my parents had left school at the ages of eleven and fourteen – but it was encouraging and enabling and the school provided as good an education as could have been found anywhere. The bombs were by that time falling, but the education persisted – disciplined and culturally broad at the hands of men, and a few women, with first class degrees from the best universities. I count myself lucky to have inherited a social system that was already providing such opportunities for those who did not come from academic, professional or wealthy backgrounds.

By means of an Open Scholarship, I went to wartime Oxford, to a society light years away from my domestic milieu and one that was already, under the impact of the war, very different from what it had been in the 1930s (Evelyn Waugh and all that!). The Oxford chemistry school at that time had been for two decades pre-eminent in the country and outstanding in the world, vying with Harvard and Berkeley. The physical chemistry laboratory alone had five or six Fellows of the Royal Society amongst its ordinary lecturers and there were almost as many in the other chemistry laboratories. It was there I early learnt an essential lesson of academic life – that many members of the staffs of British university departments can be as intellectually distinguished as its professorial head.

The Oxford Finals Honour School of Chemistry at that time was probably the most specialised course ever devised by a university. It was entirely in chemistry and lasted four years during which one did research and wrote a thesis which was then also taken into account in assessing one's final class in the Honours School. Oxford chemists at that time prided themselves, not only on excellence in their subject (so they immodestly thought), but on being wide-ranging and catholic in their interests. So I did all the usual things – I played rugby football and rowed, listened to music and went to concerts, argued about philosophy and religion and I was even once President of the English Club entertaining authors like Rebecca West and Dylan Thomas to dinner before they gave us their pearls of wisdom.

Physical chemistry appealed to me, and still does, because of its intellectual coherence and beauty – in particular kinetics, thermodynamics and quantum theory. In fact when I look back over my rather varied teaching career, I find I never actually stopped teaching or writing about thermodynamics in some context or other. For example, my last scientific book[1] on the physical chemistry of biological organization was concerned with the irreversible thermodynamics of biological processes. The research I did for my first degree and subsequently for a doctorate was in the

Oxford Physical Chemistry Laboratory where I worked with Sir Cyril Hinshelwood. He was himself a polymath – one of those wide-ranging products of the Oxford chemistry school – who by then had received a Nobel Prize for his work on chemical kinetics. He was in the same year President of the Royal Society and President of the Classical Association; he spoke and read most European languages, including Russian, and furthermore read and spoke Chinese. When I joined his team, he had begun to apply his knowledge of chemical kinetics (the study of rates of chemical reactions) to the study of the processes of living organisms. I worked on the rate processes involved in the growth of bacteria and their inhibition by certain substances. I duly obtained the degree of D.Phil. and took up a post in the University of Birmingham and in 1948 married the sister of an undergraduate friend – very conventional and it has lasted happily for over forty eight years! (We have a son, now a professor of philosophy in Oxford, and a daughter, now an Anglican priest and a project development officer for religious education).

In the 11 years at Birmingham, where I moved from being Assistant Lecturer to Senior Lecturer, I worked on something that had begun to interest me, namely the physical chemistry of DNA molecules. DNA at that time was only just becoming to be seen as a very big molecule – we now know, of course, that it has tens of thousands of units strung along two intertwined helical chains. There was some challenging physical chemistry to be done in relation to this extraordinary structure and I was able to engage in this with the simplest of equipment (e.g., a pH meter) but with a maximum of intellectual challenge. In 1952, I was in Berkeley on a Rockefellow Fellowship, at the distinguished Virus Laboratory headed by W. M. Stanley of tobacco mosaic virus fame, when James Watson and Francis Crick announced the structure of DNA in the British Journal *Nature*. Doing primarily physico-chemical work on DNA with results of interest to others in the field (we were able to ascertain that the chains in DNA were not branched and that the hydrogen bonding proposed by Watson and Crick was the only kind present in the structure), I came to be, at that time, in close contact with those working on X-ray diffraction studies and the structure of DNA.

Fortunately, I was not so emotionally involved as most of them in the events that swirled around that momentous discovery in the history of biology. For example, I remember being at an informal conference in 1953 in a small town in the middle of France (Culoz) where a French scientist (a Dr Lenormant) had his country house and had invited there a dozen or so scientists to discuss the implications of the new DNA structure. I was contributing the results of my physicochemical work. There were present in the house three Nobel-Laureates-to-be and I was able to witness the contrast and interaction of their personalities so much involved in the saga of the discovery of the DNA structure – now well known from the plethora of books that have been written about that fascinating episode in the history of science, beginning with James Watson's *The Double Helix*.

My scientific career flourished, I went back to Oxford to a Fellowship at St Peter's College and a Lectureship in the University, and there I continued to teach physical chemistry and do research in physical biochemistry. I pursued research into wider aspects of the physical chemistry of biological macromolecules. After 24 years of such work I had written some 120 papers and was running a research group with ten or twelve post-graduates and post-doctoral students. Then at the age of forty eight the Oxford scientist became a Cambridge 'Dean', the name given to the person in charge of a Cambridge college chapel, Clare College, in my case.

How did this happen and why? In some ways, Cambridge was, I suppose, the last place I expected to find myself in! So now I must tell the other story, running along alone all the time, parallel and intertwined with the one I have just told – just like the two complementary chains of DNA.

I was brought up in a typical Church of England household – typical in the sense that the established Church of England was the church my family stayed away from, except for baptisms, weddings and funerals! I was sent to Sunday School at a local church whose 'high' style of worship was disapproved of by my family (presumably it was thought to be too florid and un-English in its excesses) and later I went voluntarily to a somewhat 'lower', evangelical church, in which I was confirmed.Adolescent schoolboy evangelical fervour soon gave way to a mild undergraduate agnosticism which I shared with most of my contemporaries. Yet we all went to college chapel (indeed scholars of my college, Exeter, *had* to do so being 'on the Foundation', as it was said). At that time, in the early 1940s, it was also the accepted convention that everybody went to Chapel on a Sunday evening, then to dinner in Hall, partaking of a glass of beer and then later listened to music or poetry readings in the same Hall. I was at the college of Neville Coghill, famous later for his translations and productions of Chaucer's *Canterbury Tales*, and that had a lot to do with the cultural quality of our wartime college life (perhaps I should add that Richard Burton was a contemporary, a pupil of Coghill).

Religious and philosophical questions continuously crossed my mind. I rejected biblical literalism as naïve and the penal/ substitutionary theory of atonement (which I thought unintelligible and immoral, and I still do). The urging of such views by evangelical, 'born-again' Christians in my undergraduate days was the chief cause of my alienation from all things Christian and of the end, for the time being, of my attachment to that faith. It took me some time to find out that other ways of thinking were possible for Christian believers. One of the turning points was hearing a sermon in the University Church by William Temple, by then Archbishop of Canterbury, and the most considerable philosopher-theologian to hold that office since Anselm. I came away aware, as I had never been before, that a *reasonable* case could be made out for Christian belief and that, although I still did not embrace it, it was an intellectually defensible and respectable position. So the closed door became ajar. As a graduate student, doing the scientific research I described, questions kept pressing on me – sharpened by the transparent and undogmatic faith of my wife-to-be. How *could* one explain and account for what every scientific advance unveiled and reinforced, namely the inherent intelligibility and rationality of the natural world? Both the *fact* of its existence (the answer to the questions one asks 'Why is there anything at all?') and the manifest rationality of the natural world seemed to demand some kind of theistic affirmation to make any coherent sense of it all – and making sense of a wide range of data was just what my training and research experience were making my habitual intellectual practice. So the God-idea, you might say, pursued me, and my experience echoed that of the famous first lines of Francis Thompson's *The Hound of Heaven*:

> 'I fled Him, down the nights and down the days;
>   I fled Him, down the arches of the years:
> I fled Him, down the labyrinthine ways
>   Of my own mind'

The data, which we need to put together into some sort of intelligible and meaningful pattern, include human beings with all their sublime achievements and also their manifest degradations. By this time, it was now late 1940s. My generation had seen, if only by film and photograph, what the Allied Forces had opened up in Dachau, Auschwitz and Belsen and we had looked down into the bottomless pit of the potentiality of human evil, which the twentieth-century has seen escalate with an enhanced power perhaps more than in any other.

I tried, in my own ill-informed way, to come to grips with the problem of evil – a full intellectual solution may always elude one, thought I am now able to narrow down and specify the problem better. It certainly became clearer then, and this still seems to me to be valid, that, even if the existence of evil raises baffling intellectual questions, and it certainly does, we have been shown how evil is to be *overcome* in reality and not just in theory. I began dimly to perceive what is sublimely expressed in the concluding stanza of Dante's *Paradiso* – where he describes his final vision of God:

> 'High phantasy lost power and here broke off;
>   Yet, as a wheel moves smoothly, free from jars,
>   My will and my desire were turned by love,
> The love that moves the sun and the other stars.'[1]

It is *love* that overcomes evil and the one Creator God, whose existence as Supreme Rationality I had begun to be driven to recognise, was also, it became clearer to me, the One whose inner character is least misleadingly described as 'Love' and whose outgoing activity is an expression of that same nature that shines through the life, death and resurrection of Jesus the Christ. So my quest proceeded. Looking back at my time as a graduate student in physical chemistry I am just amazed how arrogantly I assumed I could learn little from the theologically informed minds all within half a mile of me and ploughed my own furrow, reading my own books without asking any of the learned people around me what they thought about these matters. Perhaps one has to make one's own way – however meandering, it will always be one's own and maybe there are no short cuts.

In Birmingham, I rapidly became disenchanted by the content of most sermons. Thus it was that I undertook more systematic study and, on the advice of Geoffrey Lampe then professor of theology at Birmingham University, I even managed to get a degree in theology. I was deeply influenced (and still am) by the writings of judiciously reasonable theologians – William Temple, Charles Raven, Ian Ramsey, and Lampe himself. I could not then, and do not now – and here my formation (my *Bildung*) as a scientist comes out – accept any automatic authority of church or scripture *per se*. For me, belief must meet the general criteria of reasonableness, or inference to the best explanation. This is still my position, although it is coupled with a growing awareness of our dependence on the earliest witnesses to Jesus as the Christ and of our need to sit at the feet of the men and women of God of all ages, traditions and religions.

I was relieved to discover that the much Press-besieged and battered Church of England (our part of the Anglican Communion) was theologically, philosophically and intellectually a very *broad* church, providing the space in which to move and grow, feeding, as it does, on both Catholic and Reformed traditions and influenced too by the Eastern Orthodox (and indeed the ancient Celtic) churches. It has long had the habit of emphasising the role, in the formation of a securely based and stable faith, of the use of reason based on experience in sifting both Scripture and Tradition. Its reliance on this 'three-legged stool' of Scripture-Tradition-Reason could in fact claim to be its own special distinctive feature, since other churches tend to rely more exclusively on Scripture or Tradition.

It is instructive, in this connection, and in view of my own personal synthesis of science and religion, to read what the first historian of the Royal Society wrote in 1667 about the relation of Church and science, the new natural philosophy. Remember the Royal Society had only been founded a few years before almost concurrently with the restoration of the Book of Common Prayer and of the Church of England after the Commonwealth had abolished them.

This historian, Thomas Sprat wrote:

' ... we behold the agreement that is between the present *Design* of the *Royal Society* and that of our Church [of England] in its beginning. They both may lay equal claim to the word *Reformation*; the one having compassed it in *Religio*n, the other purposing it in *Philosophy*. They both have taken a like course to bring this about; each of them referring themselves to the perfect *Originals* for their instruction; the one to the Scripture, the other to the large Volume of the *Creatures*. ... They both suppose alike, that their *Ancestors* might err; and yet retain a sufficient reverence for them ... The *Church of England* therefore may justly be styl'd *Mother* of this sort of *Knowledge*; and so the care of its *nourishment* and prosperity peculiarly lyes upon it'[3].

Supposing 'our ancestors might err' and yet retaining a 'sufficient reverence for them' seems to me just the right balance between destructive radicalism, on the one hand, and dogmatic traditionalism, on the other. So I count myself fortunate that, at that stage my quest, I had the chance of pursuing it within the ranks of a Christian church that is the reformed and the catholic Church of my own people – one that had, and still has, the habit of allowing open inquiry into the reasonableness of faith in the light of modern (in my case scientific) knowledge.

Theological study showed me something I had *not* expected, such is the myopia of the professional scientist, namely that the Christian church throughout the ages has, behind its shifting and variable facade, a very tough-minded intellectual tradition of its own, which makes the content of its thought a worthy and proper subject of university study – the message I had begun to pick up in that sermon of William Temple. Figures such as Paul, Origen, Gregory of Nyssa, Augustine, Anselm, Aquinas – amongst many others – are intellectual giants and simply cannot be ignored by any twentieth-century seeker after intelligibility and meaning.

Naturally, I always found myself relating my scientific world-view to theological perspectives. I found I could not ignore the continuity and interchange in the human being between physical, mental, aesthetic and spiritual activities and the knowledge we gain from them, all modes of our being persons. In theology, this meant I would place, and still do, a strong emphasis on the *sacramental* (which is, in the realm of theology, the concept that unites the physical, the mental, the aesthetic and the spiritual). I had for some ten years or so been what the Church of England calls a 'Lay Reader' and so had been authorised to conduct non-sacramental public worship and to preach. But this increasingly felt like trying to walk on one leg, especially as the synthesis of the scientific and Christian aspects of my life and thinking was occurring increasingly through the sacraments and the sacramental aspects of all of life. This meant I experienced a growing urge to celebrate sacramentally our unitary awareness of nature, humanity and God.

Some years before, at Birmingham, I had begun to think of ordination to the priesthood as a 'worker-priest' – that is, in my case, a 'priest-scientist' – but the move back to Oxford had put that thought into cold storage. In the event, after an abortive attempt at a change of career, and some 12 years after my beginning to think of it, I was ordained in 1971 first to the diaconate and then to the priesthood in Christ Church Cathedral, Oxford, where – it so happens – I officiate at the moment as an Honorary Chaplain and Honorary Canon.

I shared, and still share, all the average Englishman's conditioned reflexes towards, the suspicions of the clergy as a class, so I was glad to become a priest but had then, and still have, no intention of becoming a 'clergyman' (I hope I have avoided it). Fortunately this attitude coincided with the outlook of the enlightened Bishop of Oxford (Kenneth Woollcombe) who ordinated me to the 'title' of my Oxford college Fellowship – a legal relic from the mediaeval church whereby an Oxford or Cambridge college fellowship was *ipso facto* regarded as being a 'cure of souls', that is, as a pastoral charge (a salutary reminder to twentieth-century university professors?).

After ordination, I intended to continue as a priest-scientist, a university research worker and teacher in priest's orders doing my job with and alongside everyone else. And such I have always regarded myself. I would have stayed at Oxford except that Clare College, Cambridge, was looking for a Dean and offered me the post. I liked the idea of running a College Chapel that could be flexible and open, yet transmitting and educating a new generation in the incomparable liturgies and musical heritage not only of the Church of England but of the universal, that is, of the catholic church. Also, I liked the idea of a post that would allow me to do what no university faculty could : to work on the interface between science and theology. (Somehow I have always tended to be on boundaries – even in science I was between physical chemistry and biology – but this was now a larger and longer one).

My decision to go to Cambridge was not easy. Not only did I know from bitter experience how much I would feel the wrench of departure from Oxford which had nurtured me, but also for an essentially twentieth-century reason – I was half of a two-career family. My wife. Rosemary, who had been a teacher and then a headteacher had now become one of H.M. Inspectors of Schools – a unique British institution (now, sadly almost completely dismantled). Such Inspectors were then an independent body who had the role of monitoring the standards of education in the country and of reporting directly to the Secretary of State for Education. When the offer came from Cambridge my wife had her area of responsibility around Oxford – and Cambridge was some two-hours' drive away. So we faced the perennial problem of the two-career family. I did not accept the invitation from Clare College until she had been assured that she could continue in the Inspectorate, working from Cambridge.

Thus it was that for eleven years I came to teach in Cambridge University courses in the Divinity Faculty on the interaction of science and theology, and on physical biochemistry in the Biochemistry Department. Anyone who has tried to jump faculty boundary lines will realise how exceptional this was, certainly in Britain. Only a University that is both a corporate entity in itself and constitutionally also a federation of independent colleges (as are, almost uniquely, Oxford and Cambridge) could have afforded me such a possibility. Furthermore, Oxford man though I am, I gladly acknowledged the opportunities that Clare College, Cambridge, gave me of intellectual freedom to explore in depth the issues that arise for the Christian faith in a scientific age, at the same time sharing in a culturally rich environment. In this latter respect the college had (and still has) a superb mixed choir whose music enriched the chapel worship and the general life of the college – and music has been a major source of inspiration to me throughout my life.

At it happened, although Cambridge gave me the time to pursue my studies on the science and religion interface, it was Oxford that provided the goad in the form of an invitation to deliver the 1978 Bampton Lectures there. The Bampton Lecturer is, unusually, appointed by the heads of Oxford colleges, an almost totally lay (and largely agnostic!) body and not by theologians. This is curious since the eighteenth-century testator, John Bampton, a canon of Salisbury Cathedral, had prescribed that the Lecturer should *inter alia* 'confirm and establish the Christian faith' and 'confute all heretics and schismatics' and that he should not be paid a penny until they had actually appeared in print – clearly John Bampton was as shrewd as he was philanthropic! The giving of these lectures constituted a major challenge especially as the only other twentieth-century attempt to tackle the science-religion relation in this series had been undertaken by Dr Eric Mascall from a neo-Thomist viewpoint over twenty years previously. In 1979 the lectures were published[4] (and I was paid!) and they were well received, especially in the United States. But, as one German reviewer wistfully noted, they displayed the Anglo-Saxon propensity of not describing one's methodology and metaphysics before undertaking such a task of reconciliation between disciplines. It was true that, like any empiricist, like any working scientist, I had waded into the problems thinking of ways to tackle them only *ambulando* and not on the basis of any pre-determined procedure or formula.

Those lectures nevertheless did actually contain in a couple of pages an outline of my basic epistemological stances of a 'sceptical or qualified realism' and this (more definitively labelled as 'critical realism', with respect to both science and theology) I subsequently expounded in my 1983 Meldenhall Lectures at De Pauw University[5]. This stance is characterized by the conviction that in both science and theology we are aiming to depict reality through the use of revisable metaphors and models within the context of a continuous linguistic community. This view is widely held and well supported – I am not suggesting I invented it – as an interpretation of what *science* is doing and affirming, but still needs to be established for *theology* against the tides of religious fideism, fundamentalism and conservatism that seek to overwhelm the establishing of a reasonable faith that would be plausible and believable in a cultural world dominated by the sciences. However, I cannot but think that time is on the side of critical *realism* in theology since most believers in God would give up their faith if they did not think that their models and metaphors referred to and were attempting to depict the circumambient Reality that is God – just as a scientist would not endure the trials and tribulations of research if he or she did not think they were probing into a *real* natural world. Moreover, as regard the 'critical' qualification of 'critical realism', it is becoming increasingly clear that one cannot ascertain truth in theology and religion simply by appeals to the authority of sacred books or traditions, for it is simply circular for these to try to validate themselves. They cannot be self-authenticating. Their affirmations cannot void being judged by reason based on experience – that is, 'critically'.

During this time in Cambridge, I found something about myself of which I had not previously been totally aware – namely that the scientific 'me' could not be totally absorbed without remainder into the priest, even one working on the relation of science and faith. Thus it was that, because I was free from faculty pressure to publish conventional papers (this time scientific ones), I was able to explore widely, in a way I was never able to do while heading a research group, into new developments, some still speculative, in physicochemical theory that were beginning to look exceedingly promising. These developments pertained to the interpretation of the hitherto baffling complexity of living organisms and their intricate processes. This eventually – although it was a long haul, taking ten years – resulted in the publication of that scientific monograph on the physical chemistry of biological organization I have already mentioned[1]. I brought together many previously unconnected developments in mathematics, kinetics and thermodynamics and I hope made a contribution to our understanding of the wonder of biological complexity in the natural world.

There is a time for everything under the sun, and my days in Cambridge came to an end somewhat sooner than they had to so that I could return to Oxford at the end of 1984 to set up there the Ian Ramsey Centre, at St Cross College, for the interdisciplinary study of the interfaces between theology and crucial issues in contemporary culture. This was a project that had been gestating for over 20 years, every since the philosopher of religion, Ian Ramsey, who was well known for his work on religious language and eventually became Bishop of Durham, had brought together (in a sermon before the University of Oxford in 1964) the threads of the concerns of many in the early 1960s about the need for Christian theology to cooperate with other disciplines in facing up to the intractable questions that lie at the roots, for example, of new ethical problems arising from scientific and medical research and practice and of the underlying philosophical and theological issues. The fruits of that enterprise have now, at least in part, appeared in print in various forms[6]. Relinquishing the directorship of the Centre in 1988[7] gave me more time for my writing and for the nurturing of another enterprise (S.O.Sc.) to which I will shortly refer. During the period 1990–3 I was Catechist of my old Oxford college, Exeter, and had the duty of preaching regularly in its striking chapel (some of those addresses appear in Part II of this volume).

No-one engaged in working on the interface between science and religion can be unaware of the social dimension of this interaction: the communities of those engaged in the scientific and theological enterprises are estranged and alienated and each goes its own way regardless of the other. Over the years I have been able to play some part in breaking this silence, of crossing this 'no man's land' between two groups cast by many in the role of opposing armies by inherited, and false, mythologies of what happened in the nineteenth, and earlier, centuries. In the early 1970s I started in Britain informal consultations between scientists, theologians and clergy who were concerned to relate their scientific knowledge and methods of study to their religious faith and practice. This initially small group grew in numbers as it faced these increasingly complex issues and in 1975 the Science and Religion Forum was formally inaugurated at Durham. It has been meeting annually and publishing its deliberations and reviews of relevant books ever since. Parallel, though mostly smaller, groups concerned with these themes were all this time coming into existence in other parts of Europe. After an initial exploratory consultation convened by me in September, 1984, at Clare College, Cambridge, the first European conference on Science and Religion was held, with Dr Karl Schmitz-Moomann (the other initiator of the project) in the chair, at the Evangelische Akademie at Loccum in the Federal Republic of Germany on the topic of 'Evolution and Creation'[8] (*not*, be it noted, on 'creationism', which appeared in our deliberations only through its rejection). There followed a second European conference in 1988 and at the third in Geneva in 1990 The European Society for the Study of Science and Theology was formally inaugurated. All of which is immensely encouraging and of great significance for the future of religion, in general, and of Christianity, in particular, in Western society.

Much of the preceding account has referred to the concerns of the 'head'; but the 'heart' too has its reasons. Indeed, for more than 30 years I had been intuiting, instinctively discerning, that a purely intellectual dialogue between those engaged in the scientific and theological enterprises was not enough. For theology, 'theo-logy', is *ex hypothesi* concerned with words about God – and words restrict and confine. God is in 'the still small voice' and in the silences that follow louder more articulate exercises. Theo-logy cannot itself be the experience of God who is known through life in prayer, in worship, and in silence. Furthermore, I saw that the Church needs not only intellectual inquiry of the kind stimulated by the bodies I described, but it needs a cadre of committed and informed members to constitute a new kind of 'Dominican' order,[9] held together by prayer and sacrament, and committed to the life of science for and on behalf of the Church: to represent the Church in science and science in the Church. So it was that in 1987 there was founded, initially within the Church of England, a new dispersed Order, The Society of Ordained Scientists (S.O.Sc.), held together by a Rule of prayer and sacrament, to which we are committed through appropriate vows made at an annual Eucharist presided over in its first nine years by the then Archbishop of York (Dr John Habgood), as the Society's Visitor (he was himself formerly a research physiologist). The constitution has been so framed that it now includes among its members not only priests of the Anglican Communion (including six women priest-scientists) but also ministers of other churches – and also has a North American chapter. I see its future as wide open and as having great potential significance for the Church in its relation to science, technology and medicine (we have already been able to be a useful resource for it in a number of ways); and as having expanded ecumenical possibilities, for example with the relatively recently formed body, 'Jesuits in Science'.

I conclude with some general reflections prompted by this retrospect on my life, which has somehow always been spent on borderlines, whether of physics/chemistry, physical chemistry/ biochemistry, or science/theology.

First of all, *Christian belief*, or indeed any religious belief, it seems to me, will confine itself to an intellectual and cultural ghetto unless it relates its affirmations to the best knowledge we have of the world around us (and that includes the human world). This is a perennial challenge to Christian theology and to all religious belief, one that, at certain times in the past, Christian thinkers have responded to superbly and creatively. The problem today is that few theologians, and indeed few students of the humanities, have any inkling of the breadth and depth of the scientific worldview – partly because of the extraordinary narrowness of most education systems, notably that in the UK.

There is an immense work of general education needed everywhere before religious belief can begin to engage creatively with the new perceptions on the world that science now affords. Myriads of particular questions that still arise, such as:

- the nature and density of humanity in the light of their evolutionary origins;
- human needs and potentialities and the nature of the human person in the light of new knowledge from human psychology, the cognitive sciences, genetics – to name a few;
- our attitudes to nature and our influence on it;
- how to talk about 'God's action' in the light of the increasing likelihood that the universe seems to have inbuilt *self*-creative potentialities;
- human beings appear to be 'rising beasts' rather than 'fallen angels'.

And so one could go on. Such issues, and many others, cannot be ducked and will not go away.

Secondly, the *sciences*, through their range and diversity, now provide a perspective on the world whose full emotional and poetic force really needs to be conveyed by a twentieth-century Dante. That perspective indeed sharpens the questions we ask about personal meaning and intelligibility, for example: 'What kind of universe is it, that the original fluctuation in a quantum field, the primeval mass of baryons and quarks and neutrinos and light quanta, could over aeons of time by their own inbuilt potentiality and form develop into human beings who espouse values – truth, beauty, and goodness – and could become a Newton, a Mozart, Jesus of Nazareth?'

Thirdly, the *relation of science to theology* is just one of the problems of the relations of many disciplines and forms of knowledge to each other. We need today a new map of knowledge. Science shows that the natural world to be a hierarchy of levels of complexity, each operating at its own level, each requiring its own methods of study and developing its own conceptual framework, and so its own science.[10] In the light of this, I affirm that atoms and molecules are not *more* real than cells or populations of cells, or human communities, or human persons. There are *social* and *personal* facts just as there are physical and biochemical ones. In my view, the interpretation of the relation between these different levels should not be what has been called 'nothing buttery', that is, reductionism. Biology is *not* nothing but physics and chemistry; neurophysiology is *not* nothing but biochemistry; psychology is *not* nothing but neurophysiology; sociology is *not* nothing but biology. All the way up the hierarchy of complexity we see these take-over bids by the level below with respect to the level above. However, each level refers to only one aspect of reality and we need explicitly to understand the non-exclusive relations they bear to each other.

Furthermore, the scientific and theological enterprise both involve *exploration* into the nature of reality. This comes as no surprise to those studying science. However, very few people these days, (many of whom, especially politicians in Britain, use the word 'theology' pejoratively) seem to regard the theological enterprise as also an exploration into the nature of reality. But that is indeed what it is, as splendidly expressed in the opening sentence of the 1976 report of the Doctrine Commission of the Church of England on *Christian Believing*:

'Christian life is an adventure, a voyage of discovery, a journey, sustained by faith and hope, towards a final and complete communion with the Love at the heart of all things.'[11]

Let me not pretend that in my explorations I have arrived anywhere of universal significance. There is a mystery at the heart of things which requires not only all the data to be assembled together and none to be dismissed, but also the most intensive application of mind and heart and will to penetrate. The great Newton recognised as a scientist that, if he had seen further than others (he certainly had!), it was 'by standing on the shoulders of giants'. This is as true for religion as it is for science. Newton's great successor, Einstein, remarked 'Science without religion is lame, religion without science is blind'. This is indeed the leitmotif that runs through all that follows in this volume.

PART II

REFLECTIONS

Science, Creation and God

2

Natural Science and Christian Meaning

Scientists and educators of scientists, such as I myself have been, might be forgiven if we looked back with nostalgia to the palmy days of two or more decades ago when we were assigned a role by society comparable only with that of the medieval priest. Scientists not only had sources of knowledge and power not available to the ordinary person, they not only delivered the goods, but they were listened to with respect and even awe. These days, for better or for worse, have gone – and a new generation and the public in general have been quick to detect the tarnished image of science. Cracks have appeared in the sacerdotal edifice which constituted our scientific activities, cracks caused by the realisation of both the impact of technology and of the continuing need for personal meaning.

For human beings after over two centuries of unbridled expansion now face the fact that their home, the spaceship Earth, has finite resources, finite abilities to cope with pollution and a finite capacity to maintain only a limited population. The prospect fills many with gloom, not because technically these limitations present for-ever insuperable problems, but because of a deep scepticism about our human capacity to develop the will to face them politically and educationally.

With all this heart-searching and doubt eating deep into the soul of latter twentieth-century humanity, we may well ask what has happened to that *other* picture of inevitable progress which many used to see in the scientific perspective of human evolution? There is indeed still an exhilaration and a lifting of the spirit to be derived from contemplating the long, slow aeons during which there emerged from insentient matter, firstly life, then conscious life and finally the self-conscious life of humanity, of human personhood.

It is really only within the last 150 years, the second half of the 300 years of the scientific revolution and indeed mostly within the last forty, that the full grandeur and scope of what has been going on in the universe has yielded to the human adventure we call science, still the most distinctive flower (saving, perhaps, music) of our Western civilization.

Today, with the unravelling by molecular biologists in the last four decades of the chemical intricacies of living organisms, together with advances in cosmology and the earth sciences, we have a prospect as intellectually exciting as humanity has ever contemplated. The whole development of the cosmos appears to us today as an unbroken seamless web which is spun in time and in which the potentialities of the stuff of the world have gradually unfolded themselves, as conditions allowed, through the operation of purely natural laws and regularities amenable to scientific study. We can delineate a continuous sequence from a fluctuation in a quantum field, the primeval 'hot, big bang', some 10 billion years ago, with its aftermath of neutrinos, anti-neutrinos hydrogen nuclei, etc.; to the formation of heavier atoms in the galaxies; to their subsequent condensation as planets around our Sun; to the condensed masses such as the Earth, on the surface of which the chemical conditions eventually become such as to allow those complex large molecules to form that enabled self-reproducing living matter to emerge and evolve into mammals and the human-brain-in-human-body – that is, to be free, self-conscious *persons*.

Whence then all the gloom to which I have just referred? Or, if that is thought to be overstating it, why the widespread intuition that humanity is at a cross-road and has been brought there, to face unenviable decisions, by science itself? I would like to suggest to you that this present sense of uncertainty and malaise results from our failure to face up to questions which this scientific perspective itself raises, but the answers to which cannot, in principle, be found from within the resources of science, either in its concepts or its methods. These questions are about meaning – the meaning of this process of cosmic evolution and the meaning of life in such a cosmos.

The first question I would put thus: What kind of universe is it in which insentient matter, under the favourable conditions of planet Earth, can finally adopt the complex form of the human-brain-in-the-human-body, which can know, can know that it knows, and in so knowing can transcend the whole process out of which it (or, rather, he and she) have emerged? How could it come about that the possibility of persons – with their characteristics of creativity, of intellect, of love, can have been locked up in that original primeval mass of so-called fundamental particles some 15 billion years ago?

The second question is about the meaning of human life in a cosmos of *that* kind, the one we now actually find to be the case. Until *homo sapiens* the evolutionary process was effected through the random registration and expression of all the possibilities of organization inherent in matter – and this process was entirely random with respect to each new emergent form. The statistical laws of matter-energy in space-time ensured that this exploration, this realization of the potentialities of the world stuff, would miss no opportunities. We do not, we cannot, know what potentialities have been, or are yet to be realized on other worlds in other times. But on the planet Earth, we know that in human persons the stuff of the world, in becoming self-conscious, has now arrogated to itself the ability to determine its own future by itself shaping its own physical and social environment and, through education, its own response to what it produces.

So humanity is unique on this planet (and may be the only such in the cosmos) to face a future no longer determined by the statistical operation of molecular and biological laws and processes, but one determined by its own answer to the question 'What should human persons, what should human society, become?'

The natural sciences from quantum electrodynamics to the neurosciences, for all their clarity, rightly induce in us a realization of the mystery in the quality of what we know and the quantity of what remains unknown. They also induce a new humility, for we now realize that there are ultimate limits both to the smallest distances and particles we can in principle ever discriminate and the largest distances (and so time backward in the past) to which our radio telescopes can penetrate – not to mention the sheer vertigo with which our minds are afflicted as we face new concepts of matter-energy-space-time and other cosmological speculations!

For all our knowledge, indeed because of our knowledge, the questions about the meaning of the cosmos and of humanity within it, questions formerly heard only as a still small voice, now sound as the thunder of the storms which threaten to engulf us in this last decade of the twentieth-century. What is matter for? Why is there anything at all? If human beings are the ultimate product of the cosmos to date, and know the way they have come, what should they now be striving to become? Where are we going?

St Paul sensed the force of these questions that we address to the cosmos when, in his letter to the Romans, he asserted '... the creation waits with eager longing for the revealing of the children of God'.[12] In a flight of poetic fancy, he sees the cosmos as striving through its pain to give birth to that which is its consummation – the 'revealing of the children of God'.

For, to the theist, the universe is not self-explanatory – it finds its meaning in its being created by One who transcends it and us, as much as our thoughts transcend the objects of our attention. Creation by God is about the eternal relation of the created to the Creator and is not, in spite of popular mythology, in principle about what happened at a point in time. If ever it was this last, it will have been dispelled by our realization, through science itself, that the cosmos is in a continual state of evolving new forms – it is an inventive universe with respect to which God is all the time Creator, holding it in being as a created and creating entity.

But what of human beings in such a creation? I have asserted that what we should become cannot be read off from the past. The relevant, specifically and centrally Christian affirmation is set forth in the Prologue to St John's Gospel, which declares (I paraphrase) that God's action in creation stemmed from the inner life of God – it was God's own Word, God's meaning; and that this Word, this Meaning was enfleshed in the human person Jesus. That is, Jesus was God's creative Word in the flesh', so to speak. This has a double significance:

– it means that the life, death, and resurrection of Jesus the Christ is both a revelation of the fundamental purposes of God as Love (as the Christian faith has always affirmed);
– and also (of particular import for our present purposes) he is a revelation, an exemplification of what all human beings might become.

In the light of the whole sweep of the cosmic process, we can now envisage Jesus the Christ as the consummation of the creative evolutionary process. His coming has an ultimacy in that his life is the paradigm for all of us of our relation to God – a paradigm and exemplification in which God's creative purposes were brought to fulfilment. He is the point of leverage in history whereby God raises human beings, separately and together, into a new kind of human life, into a new mode of existence. This new kind of life that Jesus the Christ has opened up for us all (and which God still offers us) has two features significant for my themes.

(i) It gives *meaning to the cosmos*. For this new kind of life involves accepting ourselves as created by God, that God is Our Father and indeed Our Mother, too. We *are* created and are a part of creation and the meaning of creation for human beings is to be found only in our relation to God. For scientists themselves this could mean (amongst other things) a recovery of their joy in exploring creation, in thinking God's thoughts after and with God.

(ii) What is to be found in Jesus the Christ gives *meaning to all human life* – for we now see our role as self-conscious creatures to be so open and obedient to God, as Jesus himself, that we too become vehicles and exemplars and vessels of God's continuously creative activity in the world; that is, we are to co-operate with God in his creative action in inanimate nature, in biological life, in human society – to be, as it were, co-creating creatures, or created co-creators.

This clearly has important consequences for our attitudes towards nature and so for the role of science in society – a track we cannot follow now. However, I think that the Christian does not, should not, think that he or she has answers to many, or even most, of the baffling problems of our scientifico-technological world, though we have the duty, as a Church, to struggle with their ethical and social aspects.

What the Christian revelation does give us is the light that can be shed on all human dilemmas, the light with which the Creator suffused creation and which burst out in an unmistakable and dazzling brilliance in that person who was so open to God's creative will that he offered even his own life to draw us all into the light – and God vindicated that person by taking his very humanity into God's own life. Thereby God acted in history transposing his evolutionary creative processes on to a new plane of spiritual potentiality – a mode of existence now open, through that focal person, Jesus the Christ, to all people on spaceship Earth. 'For the creation waits with eager longing for the revealing of the children of God; for the creation was subjected to futility, not of its own will but by the will of the one who subjected it, in hope that the creation itself will be set free from its bondage to decay and will obtain the freedom of the glory of the children of God.'[13].

3

Science and God

Anyone who reads Dante's *Divine Comedy* cannot but be enormously impressed by the sheer synthetic power of his poetic imagination in integrating into one compelling narrative the cosmological, philosophical and theological insights of his times (1265–1321). Its astronomy is extraordinarily accurate, its philosophy well-informed, and its theology the fruit of a lifetime's study – and pilgrimage. It begins memorably (in the fine English translation of Dorothy Sayers and Barbara Reynolds, *see note 14*) in that 'dark wood' of the frustrations, despair and dereliction of his middle years:

> Midway this way of life we're bound upon
> I woke to find myself in a dark wood,
> Where the right way was wholly lost and gone.

In the confusions and loss of hope of our present times we know only too well what he means. But in the story, Dante is led by the figure of Virgil, the embodiment of Human Wisdom, to the very threshold of Heaven through which he is guided by Beatrice, the representative of all those agencies which have become for humanity 'the God-bearing image, the revelation of the presence of God.'[14] She finally leads him to that sublime ultimate vision of 'The love that moves the sun and the other stars'.

For most of us moderns, including post-moderns, this is a vision for which we may well yearn but do not expect to be consummated. For that human wisdom, which was personified by Virgil and which today is dominated by the natural sciences, no longer leads us so unambiguously to the threshold of the divine. The process of disruption of this unitary vision was beginning to be discerned three centuries after Dante, and half a century or so after Copernicus' *De Revolutionibus*, when John Donne, the

31

English diving and poet, writing in 1611, could expound his *Anatomie of the World* thus

> 'And new philosophy calls in all doubt,
>
> -----------------------------------
>
> 'Tis all in pieces, all cohaerence gone;
> All just supply, and all Relation:'[15]

Here we sense something of that anguish which was experienced with the breakdown under pressure from the 'new philosophy' (what we call 'science') of the medieval perception of a divinely-ordered and hierarchically organised cosmos in which humanity has an intermediate but highly significant location as a bridge between the earthly and the heavenly. We hear in this an echo of the desolation that was felt at the loss of an awareness of organic unity – 'Tis all in pieces' – the loss of a sense of a divine placement for humanity, and indeed of all things living and non-living, in an organic whole.

But neither theology nor the poets could, after the seventeenth century, stem the rising tide of a way of viewing the world that asked: 'What's there?'; then, 'What are the relations between what is there?'; and, the ultimate objective of science, 'What are the laws describing these relations?'. To implement this aim it was necessary to break things down into their constituent parts. The staggering success of these procedures cannot be over-estimated. In the course of 300 years they have altered the whole perspective of Western humanity, not least on religious belief, and on Christian belief in particular.

However, in a reputedly post-modern age, as I expect you are aware, science itself has come under attack as being sociologically and ideologically conditioned, even with respect to its actual content, and religion, of course, has long been subject to such attacks. Briefly, my position (and it is that of most practising scientists and many Christian thinkers) is that I think that both the scientific and theological communities *aim* to depict reality in metaphorical language with the use of models that are revisable.

In this perspective both science and Christian faith are engaging with realities which may be at least tentatively depicted and it is therefore entirely appropriate to ask how what scientists believe about the natural world and Christians believe about God and human nature might, or should be, related – as they always have been historically. Moreover, on the Christian faith's own presuppositions, if God has given the world the kind of being and becoming it has, then it must in some respects be revelatory of God's nature and purposes. So Christian belief should seek to be at least *consonant* with those scientific perspectives on the natural world that are well-established, as far as can be reasonably judged.

I began by referring to Dante's unified vision of nature, humanity and God. What is, then, the vista that twentieth-century science now unveils for *our* contemplation? Even those who are not scientists have, at least from television, a fairly broad appreciation of this vista – of how the universe began with some kind of fluctuation in a quantum field in an unimaginably small space, which generated an unimaginably condensed mass and expanded in some 10 billion years to our observable universe with the coalescence of matter into billions of galaxies, each containing hundreds of thousands of stars. And that on one small planet (our Earth) circulating one star (the Sun), conditions became such that self-reproducing structures could form and be living – out of which human persons have evolved. The whole has an unbroken continuity and is increasingly intelligible to the sciences. The energy and dust of the cosmos has become *persons*! What might a latter-day-twentieth-century Dante make of that?

But *we* human beings, who have come into existence through this process, seek urgently, indeed passionately, for the meaning of our existence. Thus is generated the long quest of humanity represented by the great religions of the world – the search for God. How is that search affected by our awareness of this scientific vista? Space allows only some indications of what I believe is the increasingly fruitful interplay of science and faith – so some, rather staccato, indications of a few of the outcomes of this interplay follow.

Our sense of the sheer apparent 'giveness' of the world, its obstinate contingency and actuality, is enhanced by our current awareness of the scientific vista I have just unfolded. Even the existence of the original quantum field, from which it is currently speculated that our universe 'began', calls for an explanation of some kind – the quantum laws themselves could have been otherwise. All-that-is is contingent and need not have existed at all. Hence the postulate of the existence of a *'Ground of Being'* continues to be plausible.

From the science perspective, the world exhibits an underlying unity – which may eventually be boiled down to only a few equations – yet it also manifests a remarkable diversity, fecundity and levels of complexity. The best explanation of the existence of such a world cannot but be grounded in *One* unifying source of creation and inbuilt creativity, which must constitute a *Being of unfathomable richness*, multiple in expression and outreach.

The scientific enterprise reinforces the validity of the assumption that the world has an inherent, inbuilt rationality. Hence the Ground and Source of its Being must be *supremely rational.*

The natural sciences have now led us to see that time is an aspect of the natural order, being closely integrated in relativity theory with space, matter and energy, and so, for theist, must be regarded as, in some sense, created. Moreover, in the macroscopic world, time has a direction, in which there emerge new entities, structures and processes. This reinforces the notion that the Ground of our Being is the *Sustainer and faithful Preserver* through time of all-that-is and of all-that-is-becoming.

'Ground of Being, One, of unfathomable richness, supremely rational, Sustainer and faithful Preserver' – this humanity calls 'God' as St Thomas Aquinas might have said.

The scientific perspective is of a dynamic world of entities and structures. New realities come into being, and old ones often pass away. *God is continuously creating. God is the Immanent Creator creating in and through the processes of the natural order.*

Now God is the One in whom 'we live and move and have our being', [16] so that the world is in God, but not of God, in the sense of being identical with God – the world has its own distinctive kind of being. Hence it would be more accurate also to say that *God creates the world within herself*, if we are to use personal language and so, inevitably in English, gender-definite personal pronouns of God at all.

The world seems to be finely-tuned with respect to many physical features in a way conducive to the emergence of living organisms and so of human beings. (This is the so-called 'anthropic principle' describing how dependent is the presence of carbon-based life on the precise values of many physical parameters of the observed universe). The presence of humanity in this universe, far from being an unintelligible quirk represents an inherent in-built potentiality of that physical universe in the sense that intelligent, self-conscious life was bound eventually to appear although its *form* was not prescribed. For natural selection involves propensities to complexity, self-organsiation and information-processing. Does not the very intimacy of our relation to the fundamental features of the physical world, its 'anthropic' features, together with the distinctiveness of personhood, point us in the direction of looking for a best explanation of all-that is in terms of some kind of entity that must, at least, *transcend* the personal? Hence we have good reason for saying that *God is (at least) 'personal'*, or 'supra-personal' and for using personal language to refer to God, while recognizing its inbuilt limitations.

In the light of the fecundity of evolving organic life on the Earth we can infer that *God has joy and delight in creation*, and not just in humanity alone.

We now know that it is the interplay of chance and law that is in fact creative within time. One might say that the potential of the 'being' of the world is made manifest in the 'becoming' that the operation of chance makes actual. *God is the ultimate ground and source of both law ('necessity') and 'chance'*. There is an open-endedness in the course of the world's 'natural' history which leads us to suggest that *God the Creator explores in creation.*

Certain significant features of the natural world turn out to be inherently, that is, *in principle*, unpredictable (at the quantum level and, it seems to me, in our free wills), so that we have to recognize that *God has 'self-limited' God's own omnipotence and omniscience.*

All of which has another consequence – we find ourselves having to say something like '*God took a risk in creation*' – that

God allowed Godself to be vulnerable to what the emergent entities in creation might do or become.

But the whole process involves pain, suffering and death of living organisms and if we take seriously that all this occurs as, in some sense 'in God', that God is immanently present 'in, with and under' these processes; and if God is not to become a moral enormity with us as the mere plaything of an absentee deity, then we have an intimation that *God suffers in, with and under the creative processes of the world* with their costly, open-ended unfolding in time.

All of this is but a bare outline of the opening-up of an inquiry into the newly fruitful interplay of science and faith. But I hope this gives at least a hint of how it is even more true for us today, than it was for the writer of Isaiah, chapter 40, that we can raise our voices in astonished wonder at the created order: 'Lift up you eyes on high, and behold, who hath created these things, that bringeth out their host by number … Hast thou not known? Hast thou not heard, that the everlasting God, the Lord, the Creator of the ends of the earth, fainteth not, neither is weary? There is no searching of his understanding.'[17]

4

GOD – Maker of heaven and earth

Small children sometimes ask disturbing questions. I recall one small child singing that line of a hymn which goes 'God is Three and God is One' – sudden pause – 'so God must be four'. Needless to say, that small boy is now a philosopher! One of the questions which children ask as they emerge into awareness and a sense of identity is 'Why is there anything at all?' It is, as they say, a 'good question' and one that does not go away as the child grows into the adult. It is indeed one of the most fundamental of questions and has even been given a name, the 'mystery of existence question'. Even philosophical sceptics often regard this question as central to philosophy. It seems to be an inevitable concomitant of self-consciousness, one that is raised from the very beginning of human culture – 'Why *is* there something rather than nothing?'. 'Why *is* there anything at all?'. Human beings are aware of the contingent character of their existence and of the universe as a whole – there it is in all its splendour but it does not *have* to be.

All of us seek intelligibility and we have to go on pressing our 'Why?' questions to the uttermost limits until to go any further is plain silly. Closer philosophical examination of the mystery of existence question reveals that it is certainly not meaningless and that its answer cannot be an 'explanation' in the ordinary sense of the word – we cannot look for an answer within the network of cause and effect of the natural world. But 'explanation' can mean 'that which renders intelligible'. In the light of this, belief in God as Creator amounts to the assertion that the postulate of God's existence is that kind of explanation. That is, God is conceived as that which, the One Whom, makes for intelligibility – and beauty and righteousness. God is the source of intelligibility and meaning, providing purpose and significance for all-that-is. God is the circumambient Reality, the ultimate context of all, the One 'in whom we live and move and have our being', as St Paul put it at Athens.[16]

It is in this sense of explanation that creation by God may be said to explain the existence of all-that-is. But it is not only the awareness of the contingency of existence that was the 'launching pad' for the Judeo-Christian doctrine of creation. That belief was also inextricably linked with the historical experience of the ancient Hebrews of their dependence on a transcendent Reality which they come also to identify with that Reality on which all existence depends. Thus the 'Lord God of Abraham, Isaac and of Jacob' actually was for them God the Creator, eventually seen as the only one God of all peoples. The ancient Hebrews did not think in abstract terms but in concrete images and denoted God by the name 'Yahweh' which, the scholars tell has, has the meaning of 'He who causes to be (or creates) what comes into existence', or even, 'The God who makes things happen'.

Unravelling the implications of the Biblical ideas on creation has proceeded throughout Christian history. In its developed form, the Christian doctrine of creation becomes an assertion that the world was created with time, and not in it; that the cosmos continues to exist at all times by the sustaining creative will of God, without which it would simply not be at all. The models which have been used in the past range from those stressing the distance between Creator and created (God as Maker, as King) to those stressing the closeness of the relation between Creator and created (e.g., the relation of breath to body). For Christians two other biblical images are especially significant, melding together, as they do, these two poles – they are creation as the manifestation of God's Wisdom and the expression of God's Word, that is, as proceeding from the inner life of God.

However, even with these biblical resources, we cannot avoid asking how, in what way, can we believe today in God as creator ? We now know that the world is in continual process of change in which new forms emerge, at new levels of complexity, displaying new properties – notably those of consciousness and, in humanity, self-consciousness. The processes of the world are characterized by continuity, emergence of the new, with a genuine open-endedness in certain macroscopic events.[18] Creation is still going on –

God is still crea*ting* in and throughout the events and their interactions in the actual universe science reveals. Thus, creation is
not an event at one datable point in history. It is a perennial relation of God to the world – God is *semper Creator*. This is no more
inconsistent with the world being a lawlike network of events
than is the fact that our bodies obey the laws of physics and chemistry, yet we are self-conscious, free-willing agents. We have to
conceive all-that-is as the means whereby God expresses the
divine creativity in a world increasingly describable by the
sciences. The warp and woof of the events and processes of the
world are in themselves the Creator God in action.

Today we have to recognize also that the process of creation,
the bringing into existence of new forms of matter, especially
living organisms, involves an interplay of change and necessity,
of the randomness whereby all the potentialities of matter are
worked over the givenness of the fundamental parameters of the
universe. These potentialities are written into the world by the
Creator and they are unveiled by chance exploring their gamut.
The creative role of chance operating within the necessities that
are themselves created leads one to invoke models of God's activity which express the sheer gratuitousness of God's exuberant and
fertile creation.

The created world then comes to be seen as an expression of
the overflow of divine generosity. We thereby come to see that
God takes joy in all creation for its own sake and not only in and
for the sake of humanity – as dramatically expressed in the reply
to Job when God finally answers him out of the whirlwind and
says, in effect, 'Where were you when I made the earth? Where
were you when I enclosed the sea within its boundaries or set the
Pleiades on their course?' – the implication being that God has
concerns other than those focused upon Job and his ilk. This has
the consequence for those who believe in the Creator God that all
creation is of value to God and this must be weighed in the
balance scales of any assessments we make of our interactions
with nature. The world is to be reverenced *as* God's creation.

But there is also another consequence of these reflections upon
God's creative activity. The action of God as creator while manifest in all that is going on in the world, nevertheless in humanity

becomes manifest also as actual creativity. So that when men and women self-consciously attain excellence in some purely human activity, whenever they attain a costly originality of a purely human kind, then in that attainment they are in harmony, in tune with, acting in concert with God's own creative work. This is the basis for that genuinely *Christian* humanism which has been so sadly lacking our culture this century. As Christians we must open our hearts and minds and eyes and ears to what God is both creating in nature and through the works of the humanity whom God has evolved in and evoked out of that same natural world. And we must join in this creative work, as William Blake urged: 'Let every Christian, as much as in him lies, engage himself openly and publicly before all the World in some Mental pursuit to the Building up of Jerusalem'.[19]

We are called to participate in God's creative work and to delight in God's world, to experience that 'Grandeur of God' which Gerard Manley Hopkins described in his poem of that name:

> '... nature is never spent;
>   There lives the dearest freshness deep down things;
> And though the last lights off the black West went
>   Oh, morning, at the brown brink eastward, springs –
> Because the Holy Ghost over the bent
>   Worlds broods with warm breast and with ah! Bright
>   wings.'

5

The Music of Creation

In Berthold Brecht's play, 'The Good Person of Sichuan', three heavenly visitors move like a Greek chorus, trying to find at least one apparently 'good' person in the whole world – and, when they think they have succeeded, she turns out to have maintained her good deeds only by playing a double role to keep herself alive by doubtful means, in order to have the opportunity for doing good. The play ends with a dramatic cry from this failed, but trying-to-be-good, person: it was one word – HELP! This cri-de-coeur of the human heart is evoked by intense personal, social and natural tragedies of the kind most of us scarcely know where to begin to sort out. Let us start a long way back, so that we may begin to try to unravel a little the entangled threads of our existence and to discern a little more clearly the warp and weft that underlie it.

Most of us can recall, I think, how – as we grow through childhood – we begin to acquire a sense of our self-identity and to ask 'Who am I?' and, perhaps later, 'What am I here for?' This growth in our sense of self is paralleled by a growing awareness of the world as distinct from this newly-discovered self and we wonder at the sheer givenness of the world in which we are set. Noone has expressed this sense of wonder of the child at the glory of the existence of the world around us more eloquently than Thomas Traherne:

'Is it not strange, that an infant should be heir of the whole World, and see those mysteries which the books of the learned never unfold? The corn was orient and immortal wheat, which never should be reaped, nor was ever sown. I thought it had stood from everlasting. The dust and the stones of the street were as precious as gold: the gates were at first the end of the world. The green trees when I first saw

41

them through one of the gates transported and ravished me, their sweetness and unusual beauty made my heart to leap, and almost mad with ecstasy, they were such strange and wonderful things ...'[20]

Before and behind the desolation and tragedies that we experience, there does indeed lie the sheer givenness and wonder of the world. So we are impelled to ask 'Why is there anything at all?' and, with more experience, 'Why does the world manifest the implicit rationality and beauty that the scientist and artist discern?' It is in response to such questions that we affirm that the world does not just happen to be – that it owes its origin to an ultimate Being that, in English, we call 'God'. The doctrine of creation, as it is more formally called, is not about what happened at a point in time and space, for both of these are aspects of the created order. The affirmation that the world is created is a positive response to the question why there is anything at all. To affirm that the world is crea*ted* means that it is all the time and everywhere given existence and has been endowed with being and becoming by an ultimate Reality other than itself – that Reality we name as God who transcends all that is created.

But how can we possibly think of, how can we model, the way in which God might be conceived of *as* Creator? There have, of course, been many models and images of creation in the various religious traditions, and notably the Judeo-Christian scriptures. One of the most fertile of these that I would like to develop is that of God as creative artist – of God, as it were, unfolding a pattern in time like a composer.

'Ring out, yet crystal spheres' calls Milton in his *Ode on the Morning of Christ's Nativity* and thereby reminds us of the ancient notion that the rotation of the planets made a harmonious sound humming the joy of God in creation. The idea goes back to Pythagoras who identified the numerical relation between the harmonics of a string with that between the orbits of the planets. And the ancient Hebrews, too, as we hear from the Book of Job, thought of 'the morning stars' singing together in a chorus of joy at creation: 'Whereupon are the foundations ... [of the earth] fastened? or who laid the cornerstone thereof; when the morning stars sang together, and all the sons of God shouted for joy?'[21]Today, the world revealed to us by the sciences affords an even richer and profounder context for the image of God as the supreme Creator-Composer, the incomparable Improviser.

For the panorama of the cosmos that the natural sciences has now unveiled for us is one of a greater splendour and more evocative of awe that anything that any human generation has ever before been privileged to experience and would have delighted our ancient forbears.

First of all, the sciences reveal that the world has a deep unity and yet is of immense diversity – a diversity originating in a simplicity that proves to have unimaginably fecund potentialities. From a fluctuation in the original quantum field of 10–15000 million years ago, by the subtle interweaving of four basic forces, by the elaboration of a hierarchy of structures, the complex fabric of this universe has been and is being woven. It comprises entities as different as: those most distant galaxies whose light we now see started on its way before the Earth was even formed; the icy tail of Halley's comet; the intricacies of the genetical material, the DNA, that carries the biological instructions that stamps our heredity; to the labyrinths of the human brain, the most complex material system in the known universe.

But, secondly, all this diversity-in-unity has evolved in time, itself an aspect of the created order. Time proves to be 'the locus of innovative change' as one physicist has put it – and many a musician would concur. Through the eyes of modern science, we now see the actualization in time of the undreamt-of potentialities in the first apparently simple and homogeneous condensed state from which our universe has gone on expanding. God the Creator not only gave existence to that beginning but has gone on creating in, with, and under the whole process ever since. This process involves many subtle combinations of various entities and forces and an interplay of chance and law that together prove to be essential for new forms to appear. The whole process is open-ended and immensely flexible.

How can we model this creative process and depict what God was and is up to? It seems to me that the scientist, in unveiling the overwhelmingly beautiful and subtle web woven in time by the

Creator is rather like the attentive and informed listener to the unfolding tracery and developing architecture of a musical work. Once the composer has laid down his or her pen what has been composed is subject to analysis – how it fits together vertically and horizontally, at a point in time and across time, can all be ascertained by the trained musicologist. This mirrors the activity of the scientist who analyses the natural world to ascertain its relationships through time and space.

Music is *par excellence* the art of interweaving and creating patterns in and through time so it is not surprising that it is remarkably apt as a model of the activity of God in creating continuously a world that the sciences reveal as interlocking through space and time in intricate patterns, all emerging by the operation of very few principles yet with almost cornucopian prodigality and flexibility. In music there is an elaboration of simpler units according to rules combined with much spontaneity, surprise even – and so too in the processes of creation by God.

God as creator of the natural world, which, of course, includes us, we might envisage as a composer who, beginning with an arrangement of notes in an apparently simple subject, elaborates and realises its potentialities by expanding it into a fugue by a variety of devices with always the consequent interplay of sound flowing in a derivable way from the chosen initiating ploy. Thus does a J. S. Bach create a complex and interlocking harmonious fusion of his seminal material, both through time and at any particular instant. Thus might the Creator similarly be imagined to unfold the potentialities of the universe which he himself has given to it, nurturing by his redemptive and providential actions those that are to come to fruition in the community of free beings – an Improviser of unsurpassable ingenuity. The significance of any moment in created time relates to both its past and to the potential it carries for future development – just like the instantaneous moment in an unfolding piece of music.

Music, I believe, more than any other art, is capable of communicating states of human consciousness that are otherwise inexpressible – and those works that express such states that have a universal human significance we rightly call 'great'. Any keen

listener to music, let alone performer, has on occasions had the
experience when as T. S. Eliot put it:

> [The] music is heard so deeply
> That it is not heard at all, but you are the music
> While the music lasts.[22]

In such experiences, we can be confident that we are close to the
state of consciousness of the composer. Now the music can be
reflected upon and analysed so that we see its inner relationship,
how it fits together. Both the analysis and the actual listening to
the whole are mutually enriching aspects of our experience of the
music. So it is in our relation to the natural world and its history –
the scientist, or rather the scientific community, analyses and
uncovers what is in the world and how it came to be thus.

The launching pad of that rocket which is the modern scientific
movement is often, quite justifiably, identified with that stagger-
ingly creative work – Isaac Newton's *Principia*. In that seminal
work of undoubted genius, in which he united in one original conceptual scheme the forces that operate on the earth with those that
govern the circulation of the planets, Newton regarded himself as
'thinking God's thoughts after him'. When we contemplate the
world as now revealed by the sciences we are coming into contact
with the mind of the Creator as surely as we encounter a composer's mind and consciousness, that is the composer himself, in
the composer's music. Newton, in that great work, explained
consummately some earlier observations of Johannes Kepler
concerning the solar system made at the beginning of the seven-
teenth-century, and it is to Kepler I now turn. He was a Renaissance man who shared the outlook of his contemporaries, for him:

> 'the heavenly motions are nothing but a kind of perennial
> concert, rational rather than audible or vocal ... Thus there is
> no marvel greater or more sublime than the rules of signing
> in harmony together in several parts ... so that, through the
> skilful symphony of many voices, ... [man] should actually
> conjure up in a short part of an hour the vision of the world's
> total perpetuity in time; and that, in the sweetest sense of

bliss enjoyed through Music, the echo of God, he should almost reach the contentment which God the Maker had in His Own words.'[23]

Thus it is that the modern scientist, if he is properly attuned, also hears 'the echo of God' in the music of creation with a range of insights that must evoke not only an even greater wonder than that of a Kepler or a Newton but also a profounder humility at the intricate, flexible and ever-new openness of all that to which God the Creator gives existence. Hence, with St Paul, let us sing and made 'melody to the Lord'[24] in our hearts, so that through it we may come to echo in our prayers and thoughts and lives our praise and thanksgiving to God the Creator-Composer for what he is creating in the world and seeks also to create in our lives. Thereby we together raise a paean of sound and praise to greet all those acts of creation, human and divine, in which indeed the 'morning stars sang together' and all the children of God shout for joy.

6

A Dice-playing God?

Something happens, someone gets hurt – an accident, we call it, though insurance companies, going beyond their brief, sometimes call it an 'act of God'. Rustrum Roy, then a professor of materials science at Pennsylvania State University, used to tell the following story. A plane was coming to land at Los Angeles and just as it was almost at stalling speed the plane crashed and its fuel exploded. One of those killed was a professor of physics and Roy noted the reactions of the two communities to which this well-liked man belonged. His scientific colleagues at the laboratory mourned his death, regarded it as a most unhappy accident, comforted his family and raised funds for a memorial lecture to commemorate his name and work. The Presbyterian church of which he was an elder went into paroxysms of anguish as they asked themselves 'What have we, what did he, do wrong that such a thing should have happened to him who was so much one of us?' But Jesus said: 'The eighteen people who were killed when the tower fell on them at Siloam – do you imagine they must have been more guilty than all the other people in Jerusalem? No, I tell you'.[25]

'No', says Jesus, such accidents are *not* moral judgements from God – nevertheless they can and do cause immense anguish.

– whether it is the third-century BC author of Ecclesiastes, the 'Preacher', with his Stoical theism – 'Time and chance govern all'[26]

or whether it is the crisis of faith (well before Darwin) of a Tennyson in *In Memoriam*, 'Are God and Nature then at strife,/That Nature lends such evil dreams?/So careful of the type she seems,/So careless of the single life'

– or whether, in the twentieth-century, it is the defiant courage of Bertrand Russell in ('only on the firm foundation of unyielding despair, can the soul's habitation henceforth be safely built')

– or the cool scepticism of Jacques Monod, the molecular biologist ('Pure chance, absolutely free but blind, at the very root of the stupendous edifice of evolution')

– all unite in asserting that the role of chance in nature and life is to evacuate the universe, in general, and human life, in particular, of all meaning and significance, and certainly to eliminate any possibility of the world being the creation of a purposeful God. Einstein, accepting this contrast, would not accept that quantum theory implied any inherent uncertainties, because, he said, 'God does not play dice'. So we have the stark choice: either Chance *or* God, and this is reinforced by our instinctive reactions to tragedies arising from accidents 'How could God allow this?' – or, even 'What have I, or he or she, done wrong to deserve this?' Chance or God – is that the choice?

Powerful and moving through many of those reactions I quoted are, more careful reflection indicates that, nevertheless, they are over-reactions and misrepresent the true situation. First, there is no necessary conflict in principle between purpose and chance – it is quite common in human life for human intelligence to utilise chance to achieve particular purposes. As David Bartholomew, a professor of statistics, has put it, when discussing what are called stochastic processes 'the aggregate effects of highly random processes may exhibit regularities of different kinds in areas where intuition is an uncertain guide'.[27] In the theory of games, in sampling surveys, in so-called random testing, again and again human beings utilise 'chance' to effect their purposes.

Second, we have come to realise that, over a wide range of the natural scene, chance operates always within a lawlike framework and it is the combination of chance and law that is creative of new forms. If rigid Law prevailed, the universe would be like a gigantic clock, for ever repeating the same cycle of patterns and forms. If pure Chance alone prevailed, nothing could ever exist long enough actually to be anything definite. It is the operation of chance in a lawlike framework – the combination of the two – which is creative of new forms of existence.

Thirdly, we have to recognise also that nature manifests, mainly (but not only) in natural selection, a propensity towards complexity, self-organisation, information-processing and storage, sensiti-vity, awareness, consciousness and self-conscious-ness. The dice are loaded for these to appear – and the only actual form of their concurrent appearance known to us, at present, is intelligent, self-aware, human persons.

God has created through the interplay of chance and necessity, or law. He is the God OF chance, for this is the only way even God could have brought into existence conscious, free creatures who live in a world regular enough for them to act in and to take responsibility for their decisions – and so to grow and mature as persons.

What, then, are we to say of that story I recalled about the death of that physicist in the plane accident? What, then, in the words with which John Donne assails heaven, of:

'All whom the flood did, and fire shall o'erthrow,
All whom warre, dearth, age, agues, tyrannies,
Despair, law, Chance, hath slaine'?[28]

What we have to recognise is that there is an intrinsic, ineradi-cable element of chance operating in the world and that, but for its operation, we could not be here at all as conscious, self-conscious, free-willing, sentient persons. To will the end, God wills also the means. The absorption of a quantum of energy that can disrupt a growing cell and lead to a cancer is the very same process by which those mutations have occurred on which, to use Monod's phrase, 'the stupendous edifice of evolution' is built.

We live in a milieu that, in spite of all conceivable technologies and all the blandishments of the insurance companies, can never render us immune from the 'changes and chances of this fleeting world'. Were we to be so cocooned, we could never become or grow as persons. Many of the circumstances of our lives were not and are not under our control. Our psychological and spiritual health depends on our recognising this. For we live by responding to challenge. It is in the fortifying and enriching of our responses to whatever befalls us that we encounter the God who made us for communion with God's own self and who is more concerned for our ultimate welfare that we can ever be ourselves.

The natural, including the biological, accidents and calamities that happen to us are not specifically willed by God but are the consequences of being alive at all. The words of Jesus again: 'The eighteen people who were killed when the tower fell on them at Siloam – do you imagine they must have been more guilty than all the other people in Jerusalem? No, I tell you' ... and, he goes on, to command 'Repent'. That is, change yourself around, alter the direction and aim of your lives – set your course towards your Creator.

God can then, and only then, give us the strength and resilience and that unique gift of his grace – hope – to face any calamity, any accident, major or minor. Only a steady and regular waiting upon God, only such a quiet and persistent attempt to live in the presence of God can bring fruit out of the most barren situations. Then, whatever the circumstances, whatever happens to us, we can rest in the presence of God and know that all is well and we will not be overwhelmed. This is the experience of those who have tried it – like the word which Lady Julian of Norwich heard in her experience of God six centuries ago:

' ... this word: "thou shall not be overcome" was said full clearly and full mightily for ourselves and comfort against all tribulations that may come. He said not "thou shall not be tempted, thou shall not be travailed, thou shall not be afflicted", but he said, 'thou shall not be overcome.' God willeth that we take heed to these words and that we be ever strong in sure trust in weal or woe. For he loveth and enjoyed us, and so he willeth that ye love and enjoy him and mightily trust him and ALL SHALL BE WELL.'[29]

7

God's World and Ours

Just after lunch (our time) on Monday, 13 April 1970 all was still relatively normal in the routine of the three men aboard Apollo-13, over 200,000 miles from the Earth. But, within a few minutes it was quite clear that they had a serious problem, for an oxygen tank had exploded. For them the 'shortest way home was the longest way round' and their trajectory passed behind the 'dark' side of the moon away from the Earth, and from there they saw Earthrise over the horizon of the moon – and they saw it in its bright blue and white beauty, wreathed in cloud and glistening by the light of the sun against the black void of space. The photographs they (and others) took are part of the imperishable memories of our times for they, and we through them, began to see the Earth as a space ship – and the very plight of the astronauts perhaps planted the seed of a general awareness of the vulnerability of 'Spaceship Earth'. Today, almost daily newspaper reports of new kinds of global warming, of pollution and scarcities in non-renewable resources of material and energy serve to reinforce that dramatic, and beautiful, initiation into our newly-won global awareness. A new literature on the environment has burgeoned that is astonishingly wide-ranging, from the romantic and hippy to the sober and governmental.

Let us be clear what it is that environmental science, the science (ecology) of our planetary home is telling us about the complexity of its systems. The energy source for all living organisms, including *homo sapiens*, is the sun. All plants and animals live in complex systems consisting of many crossflows and exchanges of energy and matter in various chemical forms, of baffling complexity. These 'ecosystems' and their ramifications and mutual interlocking relations are only partly understood. Those of our characteristics which render us distinctive, indeed unique, do not in any way place us outside the system. Indeed the compounding of population and of technology has suddenly within recent decades accelerated to awake us to an inescapable new fact – that we have the capability of rendering unstable the ecosystems of the Earth through the massive doses of technology which have been injected into it since World War Two. For almost everything we do to these natural systems for our own benefit is of such a kind and has such global effects that we are forced into becoming the managers of the Earth. The spaceship Earth, which is our home, shows symptoms of becoming crippled in a way no less than that of the three astronauts who saw Earthrise from the moon.

It has become increasingly clear that one of the vital components in the ecological situation we now face is the set of values we regard as operative in the process of making public and private decisions on the ecological data. To such questions concerning our relation to nature (both what it is and what it ought to be) the understanding of nature *as* creation is, I would claim, acutely relevant. So, we ask about the relation of belief in God and 'ecological values'. Are they connected? Does any distinctive attitude to nature follow from belief in God?

Scholarly labours identify the following main features in the biblical (primarily Old Testament) understanding of nature and of humanity's relation to it:

> creation is good, creation is ordered and creation is of value to God;
> nature is not to be worshipped for its own sake, is revalued and is perceived historically;
> our place in nature is to exercise 'dominion'.

This 'dominion' is one that is accorded us under a delegated authority from God who is the Creator of both ourselves and that over which we are given this derived 'dominion' and which, independently of us, has value to God as his creation. The *locus classicus* of this concept is, of course, Genesis 1, v.26: 'Then God said, 'Let us make man in our image, after our likeness; and let them have dominion over the fish of the sea …' This use of 'dominion' is related to ancient concepts of kingship which emphasis a caring kind of dominion exercised under authority on behalf of those over whom dominion is exerted. The Genesis myth therefore describes human beings as exercising the leadership of a monarch of creation. Human beings are accountable and responsible. But (the Biblical myth goes on to elaborate) although we are made in the 'image and likeness of God', we are in a state of rebellion. We use our freedom to succumb to the temptation to 'be like God, knowing good and evil'.[30] Our relation to nature is not one of pastoral 'dominion', regal and caring, but one of contention and opposition. We still stand over nature but by the exercise of our power we can (and do) disrupt the created order.

Christians value creation on these same grounds but they have, in fact, an even stronger reason for positive affirmation of both the reality and the worth of the created order – namely, the doctrine of the Incarnation. For if God was able to express the nature of his own being, explicitly in and through the life, death and resurrection of the human Jesus, then the world of matter must be of such a kind not only to make this possible – but also to have value to God as such. In the Christian understanding, the world of matter has both the symbolic function of expressing his mind and the instrumental function of being the means whereby he effects his purposes, that is, the world is a sacrament or, at least, sacramental. As F. J. A. Hort, the nineteenth-century Cambridge New Testament scholar and natural scientist, put it: 'All Christian life is sacramental. Not alone in our highest act of communion are we partaking of heavenly powers through earthly signs and vehicles. This neglected faith may be revived through increased sympathy with the earth derived from fuller knowledge, through the fearless love of all things'.[31]

In themselves, that complex of ideas about nature, humanity and God we have called the Judeo-Christian doctrine of creation far from instilling attitudes inimical to harmony with nature provides a strong motivation, to those who hold them, towards action based on desirable ecological values. An awareness that we stand before God as our Creator, with power over, and immense responsibility for, the rest of the created world provides us with the strongest possible motivation to act for the future good of humanity and for the whole ecosystem. Responsibility to *future* generations takes on an added gravity when we realise that we hold the balance of the Earth's ecosystems in trust, and that we are answerable for them to its Creator. But just as there are good grounds for amplifying and enriching the Judeo-Christian doctrine of creation, in the light of the sciences, so we must now reconsider our role in the creation from a newer perspective.

The traditional ideas that I have just outlined, are based on an emphasis on God as transcendent creative agent, and have generated such terms as 'vicegerent', 'steward', or 'manager' to represent our role in relation to nature. However, these terms, in modern English, still introduce a nuance of 'domination' into the biblical concept of 'dominion' and do not adequately convey the 'caring' component in ancient ideas of kingship. Our enriched understanding of the doctrine of creation in the light of the sciences, especially evolutionary biology, now impels us to stress particularly that God the Creator is immanent as agent in a world that God is still creating. This immediately suggests that we should respond to nature with a respect of the same kind as a person accords to his or her own body and those of other persons as being the expression of those other 'selves' – as if the world's relation to God is analogous (and only analogous) to that of our bodies to ourselves. Our attitude to nature should show a respect which is transmuted into reverence at the presence of God in and through the whole of the created order, which thereby has, as it were, a kind of derived sacredness, which again is to say that the world is sacramental.

Indeed our role may be conceived as that of priests of creation, as a result of whose activity, the sacrament of creation is reverenced. We alone are conscious of God, ourselves and nature, and so can mediate between insentient nature and God. We alone can contemplate and consciously offer the action of the created world to God. As George Herbert expressed it:

'Man is the world's High Priest: he doth present
the sacrifice for all: while they below
Unto the service mutter an assent,
Such as springs use that fall, and winds that blow'[32]

Similar attitudes have been attributed to pragmatic biologists who, having reflected on ecological complexity, regard it as an act of vandalism to upset an ecosystem without good cause for doing so. But biology *per se* seems able to generate only a human self-survival policy towards nature, whatever the sympathies of individual biologists. We need to explore the implications of seeing the natural world as being created by God. We need to see God as actively unveiling his meaning, of speaking his word, to that part of his creation, ourselves, capable of seeing and hearing him. This allows us to see the natural world as a *symbol* of God's meaning: this understanding is, indeed, included in the concept of the world as a sacrament and suggests further that we are the interpreter of creation's meaning, value, beauty and destiny. We alone in the natural world read, articulate and communicate to others the meanings we read and in this we alone have a prophetic function. Like Hamlet's players, our role is 'to hold, as t'were, the mirror up to nature'.

More precisely, we must see the world as continuous creation, for creation is still going on. And we too, find ourselves with creative capabilities, so we are faced with the choice of cooperating in the continuous creative work of God or of disrupting it. We now have the opportunity of consciously becoming *co*-creators with God in his work on Earth, and perhaps even a little beyond its edge In the doctrine of creation in the light of the incarnation we have the basis for a genuinely Christian humanism, in which all human excellence is seen as human beings making their distinctive human contribution as co-creators to that ceaseless activity of creation which is God's action in and for the world.

Yet there is a cost, for the life and death – in conjunction with the teaching – of Jesus, provides a profounder revelation than that offered by the evolutionary process of the truth that God as Creator suffers in and with his creation. So we cannot expect to participate in the creative process, to be, as we said, co-creators with God, without cost and without love. Too much contemporary ecological discussion has been in terms of a sophisticated projection of the human desire for survival – not wrong in itself, but inadequate for providing the larger perspective the mounting crisis demands. Furthermore, since the sphere of God's creative work is always from the present into the future, to aspire to be co-creators with God necessarily involves acting for the *future* good of both humanity and the Earth's ecosystem. For us to see ourselves as co-creators with God therefore provides a powerful motivation to act for the future good.

To be co-creators with the 'living God', who always actualises in his creation new possibilities, previously unimagined humanly speaking, is to be prepared always to adjust creatively and deliberately to the changes necessary for God's purposes to be fulfilled – and this is bound to be a sacrificial, costly process of love in action. I cannot pretend, at this point, that how we are to become such co-creators with God, and how this could be possible at all, seeing what we are, does not raise profound questions to which, it seems to me, the whole resources of the Christian faith are the response. Nevertheless I hope that this understanding of God as Creator that I have been developing is of such a kind that it might unite all those who are engaged in the 'Long Search' for God; and that such an understanding might enable people of widely diverse kinds of belief in God to join in that perpetual *Benedicite* which, no doubt, the morning stars first sang together when the sons of God shouted for joy:

> O, All ye Works of the Lord, bless ye the Lord:
> praise him, and magnify him for ever.
> O, ye holy and humble men of heart, bless ye the Lord;
> praise him, and magnify him for ever.

Communication from God?

8

Light for the Dark Ages

'To be a light to lighten the Gentiles' the church sings in the *Nunc Dimittis* every Sunday evening. We, by and large, are the so-called 'Gentiles', those outside ethnic Israel to whom the light has been extended from the heart of that ancient religious tradition by the coming of Jesus the Christ.

However today, in the West, or at least in Western Europe, that light radiating out from the stable of Bethlehem, that light which (according to the Prologue of St John's Gospel) was the life of human beings, that light still shines in darkness and is little more comprehended today in Western society than it was in the first century of the Christian era. For although Christianity is still spreading, it is doing so everywhere except in the secularised West, where Christian adherence has virtually collapsed into a remnant, certainly in much of Northern Europe.

It is beginning to be recognised that there has been a kind of watershed in religious consciousness in the last two decades in this country, at least. Even as late as 1963, at the time of the publication of John Robinson's *Honest to God*, it was possible for as many in the Western world as were interested to learn from the media what was at stake in the debate and to join in, if they wished. But since then the activities of publishing houses and of other agencies which educated the general public in Christian matters have sharply declined, so that, apart from occasional efforts by the BBC, the genuine inquirer hears only a travesty of the truths of Christianity and of genuine debates in Christian thinking. (Recall, as just one example, the treatment in the tabloids of David Jenkins when Bishop of Durham).

Then, by way of reaction, the loudest voices claiming to speak for the Christian faith are those of fundamentalist, authoritarian and charismatic groups who offer simple, inerrant and unquestionable so-called 'truths' – so alienating the many in our society

who are starved of that substantial and nourishing diet which critical minds require for commitment with integrity. For our society
is full of several generations now of wistful agnostics who have
never had the chance of even hearing of the comprehensive intellectual force of the Christian gospel. So the light that is meant to
lighten us Gentiles is diffuse, distorted and dimmed by the
vaporous (and vapid) fog that the media incessantly cast over our
minds.

This low public level of discourse has not only driven out
Christianity as the *lingua franca* of our communal aspirations, but
has also led to a kind of 'privatization' of religious belief, so that
Christian groups are widely thought to be held together by an
ideology that is irrelevant to any general truth sought by everyone
else. What a long way this is from St Paul who could write to the
Gentile Romans that 'all that can be known of God lies plain
before their eyes; indeed God has himself disclosed it to them.
Ever since the world began his invisible attributes, that is to say
his everlasting power and deity, have been visible to the eye of
reason, in the things he has made'.[33] Paul is here appealing to a
general revelation of God which all can discern in the nature of
things. But he also appeals over and beyond this general to a
special and particular revelation that comes from the good news
(the 'gospel') which God has communicated through the prophets
and uniquely in Jesus the Christ. It is good news about the power
of God to heal and make whole, make wholesome, make healthy
human beings – which is what 'salvation' means in the New
Testament.

I suspect that it is just here, at the idea of 'revelation', that late
twentieth-century Westerners encounter the real stumbling block
to faith – an opaque screen which fatally dims the light of the
Gospel almost to the point of extinction. We all know about
human communications, so essential to our being fully persons –
but what of God's supposed exchanges with humankind? How
can God, as it were, speak to us, communicate with us? How can
we see the light coming from him as we stand on the verge of
what many are discerning as a new dark age in the West for
Christianity, with its diminished resources? Is it intelligible that
God can communicate with us; if so, how?

To respond adequately to this question we need already to have answered another, namely, 'How, if at all, does God act in the world?' It has become increasingly problematic for us in our times to answer this question in the confident manner of earlier generations. For we have become accustomed to regarding the world as comprising processes that are increasingly intelligible to the natural and human sciences and which display certain regularities, while – we have recently had also to recognize – in some cases having an inherent openendedness that is the basis of their inbuilt creativity. Creative persons with free will – human beings – have evolved by and in these processes which go on in the presence of God, that God in whom 'we live and move and have our being'. God is that all-pervading Reality that surrounds all-that-is and who is present to all created beings and entities. Because God is present to all created realities in their totality as well as in their particularity, God – and only God – is able to be a constraint on the total system of all-that-is. Thereby God can make some particular patterns of events happen rather than others. These particular events, or sequences of events (that is, histories) are never observed by us to infringe any regularities that the sciences and other sources of human knowledge might have discerned. Nevertheless the events are what they are because they express the intentions of God and so are personal acts in that sense. Such a kind of constraint is called 'whole-part' because it exerts its influence through the constraints which the system as a whole exerts upon its constituent parts. Such a mode of influence is entirely intelligible to us nowadays from experiences of many similar situations in the natural and social world in which the units that make up a complex whole are constrained to act in particular ways by their participation in the system, but never abrogating their own individual rules. Such systems vary from the convection of a heated liquid to the way that thoughts, states of the human brain as a whole, effect individual actions.

So, in a way, God is to the world as we, in our consciousness as personal agents, are to our bodies. Without pressing the analogy too far (for God transcends the world in a unique sense), it is worth noting that some of our actions – some gestures, body language, etc. – are more distinctive and characteristic of us, of our inner intentions and selves than spoken languages. They show more clearly what we really are – and our friends, and enemies, could tell us this better than we could ourselves!

In an analogous way, I am suggesting God communicates to us through what he has created, through the actual processes and patterns of events of the world, including those going on in human brains – and for us the most significant will be those to be found in the personal and in the history of persons. So we can intelligibly look for a general revelation of God in, as St Paul says, 'the things that are made', which includes general human experience.

Furthermore there are, from time to time, particular persons, associated with particular concatenations of events, through which God has showed his hand more specifically and explicitly. One such was the archetypal and seminal event for the consciousness of the ancient Hebrews when Moses is related[34] as having experienced at the burning bush the ineffable holiness of God to be worshipped as ultimate Being and having heard God named as: 'I am that I am' or, more accurately, 'He who causes to be, creates' or, even, 'He who makes things happen'. God is still communicating through the web of created things, mediated by sight and sound and impressed upon human brains. So these special revelations are but a particular form of general revelation.

In a religious tradition such as that of the people of Israel and then the Christian church, such seminal experiences are re-lived and communicated, and handed down, in what we call a tradition. This process has a sifting and winnowing effect and some survive and continue to be valued and others are later superseded. For God is involved in a continuous dialogue with humanity through both general and special revelation and he conveys to humanity at any one time what it is capable of bearing and receiving at that time in the light of its previous experience and current perceptions. He does not go too fast for us and the Bible is full of false starts and dead ends. So it is not surprising that as we read this ancient literature of what was at first a nomadic society, and then agricultural, and pre-Christian and certainly pre-scientific, we read things we cannot believe to be historically factual, or that are morally repulsive. God had to communicate with people as they actually were and more careful study reveals how at each point a further insight is gained, preparing for the time when the Word could become flesh of a human person.

Moreover the dialogue has not stopped. God will seek to communicate with us through every resource that the tradition has handed on to us and through our own specific experiences and psyches. In such communication the role of symbols and of the archetypes that Jung discovered undoubtedly play a large part, along with words, events and aesthetic experiences. So it is not surprising that, as the Alister Hardy Research Centre in Oxford has discovered, there is in Great Britain strong evidence that a wide variety of people have had experiences of an awareness of a benevolent power that appears to be partly or wholly beyond, and far greater than, the individual self – which because of the cultural situation I described at the beginning the same people are often reticent to name as 'God'.

Thus the dialogue of God with humanity continues. What is handed down, what we call the 'tradition', is not a set of propositions engraved in stone that represent eternal once-for-all truths. What is handed down is the experience that God is faithful and never ceases his dialogue with humanity in order to renew and restore to humanity what God wills for our welfare and fruition. The light *does* still shine in the darkness, even of our own times, and what is required of us is that we turn our eyes to focus on it – and so comprehend it.

For there is, at the end of the day, no way to discern this light except by following the advice of the Psalmist

Be still and *know* that I am *God*[35]

9

Fountain and Well of Truth?

A college preacher, desperate for a sermon, indeed any parish priest in the same predicament, might well – though perhaps today a little inadvisedly – resort to the *Book of Homilies* published in 1547. It contains sermons for those in that not unfamiliar tight spot. Amongst its offerings it contains a sermon written by Thomas Cranmer, the Archbishop of Canterbury, in 1543 entitled *A Fruitful Exhortation to the Reading of Holy Scripture.* In that sermon Cranmer describes the Bible as 'the fountain and well of truth'. For him it was so in 1543, but can it be so for us over 450 years later? In particular, can what we call the Old Testament ever again be a fountain and well of truth?

Can the Old Testament be a source of truth

    – in the light of the critical study of its text (indicating multiple authors and editors of many of the books sometimes over centuries)?
    – in the light of analysis of its cross-connections with other literature of the ancient Middle East and so of its multiple ethnic origins?
    – in the light of archaeology and other sources that demonstrate not a few historical inaccuracies (though some exact reports as well)?
    – in the light of anthropology which shows its customs and beliefs to belong to a very definite stage in the general cultural and religious development of humanity?
    – in the light of science which shows it to have false beliefs about the natural order that were common to its times?
    – finally, in the light of what is clearly objectionable morally and religiously in many of these ancient stories? One could cite the trickery of Jacob who twice deceives his brother Esau in obtaining the latter's inheritance and their father's

blessing and yet, we are told, is the one whom God elects as the ancestor of a God's chosen people; or the awful story in the Book of Judges of how a woman, Jael, offered the fleeing general Sisera rest and refreshment only to break the laws of hospitality by murdering him with a mallet and tent peg while he slept – and this is celebrated as a triumph of God over his enemies.

Clearly earlier ideas of the verbal inspiration of every word of the Bible, in this case the Old Testament, and of its verbal infallibility will just not stand up to examination. Yet, in spite of this, some people insist on saying 'This is the Word of the Lord' after every reading from the Bible. Saying this can have such tragi-comic effects as that of the Old Testament reading in the Alternative Service Book on the Sunday before Lent which concludes a story about a man who broke the Sabbath laws, by picking up sticks, with the words from the Book of Numbers, chapter 15: 'The Lord "said to Moses, This man must be put to death ..." So they took him outside the camp, and all stoned him to death, as the Lord had commanded to Moses' – 'this is the Word of the Lord'! Apart from such inanities in the use of this phrase, it is not even a biblical use for in the Old Testament it is confined only to major pronouncements by the prophets.

And yet this cannot be the whole story, for many of us treasure in our memories sublime phrases and even whole passages of the Old Testament – and who, for example, could not but be impressed by the selections set to music in Handel's *Messiah* or in Haydn's *Creation*? However being selective is not the answer to the question of the use of the Old Testament today by a twentieth-century Christian, for we give it a much higher place than that in our liturgy and theology. So we have a problem – and a challenge.

Firstly, and briefly, let us remind ourselves of some facts. What *we* as Christians call the Old Testament is really the Hebrew Bible (though part is in Aramaic). It is really an anthology of the most significant works of the culture of the people of Israel. How this particular anthology came to be selected – and so regarded as 'scripture' by those of the Jewish faith – is a complex story.

Indeed it only reached a definite form about the time that the New Testament was being written. It contains what was formally called the Law, the 'Former Prophets' (actually the histories, which shows something about how the people of Israel viewed history), the 'Lesser Prophets' (what we would call prophecy) and the 'Writings' – everything else. Within this formal classification its prose actually contains: historical texts (the court history of David, concerning the events in the first 80 or so years of the first millennium BC, is one of the earliest pieces of continuous historical chronicle available to us in any culture), short stories, sagas (a type of folk literature, oral in origin, loaded with meaning and significance), laws, wisdom literature, prophecy (interpretation of current events). And, of course, it is saturated with poetry – devotional poems, love poems, laments, victory hymns, some whole books contain nothing else, for example the Psalms and the Song of Solomon. Indeed a very loose kind of anthology spanning 900 years from the eleventh century BC to the second century BC, from the taunt song of Deborah (following the episode in the tent) to the prose parts of the *Book of Daniel*. The variety of kinds of writing in this anthology is altogether remarkable. It might well be thought to be something like the English section of the Library of Congress. However, this would be a superficial view for it remains in what we call the Bible because it was all thought to have some significance in spite of its very contents showing that it depicts and was written by very imperfect human beings, as our brief excursion into the morality of many Old Testament stories indicated. There is a real unity amongst these disparate texts because of its strongly allusive character; that is, it represents an authoritative tradition that was both national and religious and is in continual cross-reference to itself. It is in continuous dialogue with its own past and not only often re-writes and recasts it from a new perspective but quite often contradicts it overtly. The whole constitutes a cumulative process – the 'tradition' is (conveniently forgotten by the conservatively inclined) one of constant confrontation of the present with the past and a sometimes anguished revision of attitudes – as superbly exemplified in those most profound reflections on human suffering, the Book of Job and the 'servant songs' of Isaiah evoked by the desperate experience of the Exile to Babylon of the people of Israel.

Just at there are many layers of meaning in any great work of art – and many of the books of the Old Testament *are* that – and just as there are many levels of significance in it as a whole, so its importance for us today can be adduced on several levels.

Firstly, the Old Testament is of immense cultural significance in our civilisation. Along with the classical culture of Greece and Rome it has been one of the great formative influences upon our attitudes, ethics and beliefs. Principles of justice for the underdog – the option for the poor, the stranger and the weak in society – stem directly from the prophetic call to the people of Israel, in the sixth to eighth centuries BC, that God requires social justice rather than religious observance, beginning with that stark prophet of the mid-eighth century BC, Amos, who indicted his people for selling 'honest folk for silver and the poor for a pair of sandles'[36] and prayed that justice should 'flow on like a river and righteousness like a never-failing stream'.[37] References to the Old Testament abound throughout English literature (and indeed all Western literature) – it has been a supreme source of inspiration for poets, novelist and playwrights into the twentieth century (T. S. Eliot would be unintelligible without knowledge of it). Almost as important for our own times is that it is the common root from which stem the three major monotheistic religions of the world, Christianity, Judaism and Islam – and knowledge and a sharing in our common roots cannot do anything but good for relations between members of those cultures and faiths.

Second, it must be read for its sheer quality as literature and, as English speakers, we are fortunate in having a supreme and classical expression of the English language in the Authorised Version, the King James Version based on William Tyndale's magnificent and sacrificial work – one of the most formative influences on our language, probably the most formative influence (just as, incidentally, Luther's German translation was on the development of German). The role of story-telling in our discourse about God has been a recent emphasis in theology but those more directly concerned with literature have also re-discovered the literary riches of the Old Testament. In a recent 'Literary

Guide to the Bible', edited jointly by a professor of Hebrew and a professor of English literature, the Preface states: 'Sometime in the latter part of the second millennium B.C.E., the spiritual avant-garde of the Hebrew people began to imagine creation and creator, history and humankind, in a radically new way. This radicalism of vision … generated certain underlying patterns of literary expression in the centuries that followed … [in poetry and in prose] the imaginative recurrence, for all the diversity, to the bedrock assumptions of biblical monotheism about the nature of reality weaves tensile bonds among the disparate texts. This endlessly fascinating anthology of ancient Hebrew literature was … on its way to becoming a book'[38]

Thirdly, of course – and I've left its most obvious and most significant feature to the last – the Old Testament enshrines the faith in which Jesus was brought up and to which he remained utterly committed. Recent scholarship has come to emphasize as never before the Jewishness of Jesus, something that we have often preferred to forget:

– his regular practice as a faithful Jew of the prescriptions of the Law, while (like the best of the Pharisees) pointing out their true inner meaning;
– his adherence to the teachings of the Pharisees who, in spite of the bad press given them by the evangelists, constituted a spiritually-oriented reforming movement in first-century Jewish religion;
– the essential Jewish content of his message about the restoral of the kingdom of God, and the renewal of the temple;
– his deliberately choosing 12 apostles corresponding to the 12 tribes of Israel;
– and so and so on.

A very great deal of what we as Christians believe about God and his relation to humanity and the world we derive from Jesus and the early church who knew only the Old Testament as scripture, as authoritative writings enshrining their tradition. And none of it was written as a prelude to Christianity, in spite of the gloss that

Christians have subsequently tried to impose on it. Christian faith gives a central place to the teaching, life and work of the historical Jesus – and his God was the God already made known to Israel.

We have therefore in the Old Testament a unique and irreplaceable account of a cumulative process in which the dialogue between humanity and God has occurred and has been recorded in accounts of the wide-ranging experiences of a whole people through many centuries. These encounters in history which are interpreted as interactions with God, even in the most secular and mundane stories and histories, make sense because they are given a framework of meaning already created by previous encounters remembered in the tradition. So the interaction with the realities of existence through which God's presence is recorded as mediated is an interaction with One whom their forefathers have already encountered both in judgement and in mercy. The Old Testament records this experience and these encounters for us and we are simply arrogant if we fail to be refreshed by these deep waters. The older idea of 'progressive revelation' which so appealed when the difficulties with the Old Testament were first frankly recognised has given way to the notion of the Old Testament as a cumulative process. As in the history of an art form, such as music, one cannot really talk of progress – each period has qualities and insights from peak experiences and seminal figures that remain for always an inspiring source to succeeding generations, even as they develop their own insights to meet the challenges of their own times. So it is also with the history of the often fraught dialogue between God and humanity. It is that about which we learn from the Old Testament. For even when we can no longer say that the Bible *is* the word of God, each and every word inspired and infallible – we can be sure that it contains God's word to humanity.

So – 'The fountain and well of truth'? The Old Testament is like a well, deep and hard to get at, from which the truth has often to be extracted laboriously by study using all the tools of scholarship. But it is also like a fountain, fresh and accessible, with its own power to communicate truth to the receptive mind.

'Do not suppose', said Jesus, 'that I have come to abolish the law and the prophets; I did not come to abolish, but to complete'[39] – that same Jesus on whose lips on the Cross were the words of a psalm (22) and of whom it could truly be said that unless thy law had been his delight, he would have perished in his affliction.[40]

10

Where shall Wisdom be found?
(Job 28.12)

There are many who, in their first days at the university or in any new job, find themselves baffled and confused when confronted with the multitudinous and various decisions that have to be made so many times a day on so many matters. There are many immediate problems to sort out. But then there are the more strategic ones and, looming over all, 'How is this all fitting into what I might do in the future – and how does that fit into my general aims in life?'

The ability to cope with such questions, to make poised, careful and mature judgements in practical life was what was constituted 'wisdom' in one tradition of the biblical literature represented in the book of Proverbs, in the Psalms – and in parts of the book of Job. But the meaning of the word 'wisdom' in this narrower, practical sense, gradually became enlarged. For the ability to make such judgements surely itself depends on knowing what really is the case, and so wisdom came to include knowledge of the nature of things – and this implied mastery of intellectual skills. However the process of expansion of the idea and of the meaning of the word 'wisdom' could not stop there. For 'wisdom' came to include knowledge of the reality which was humanity, human life, purpose and destiny and so to refer to appreciation of the totality of the finer things of life – intellectual, aesthetic and religious.

Wisdom, so described, seems beyond our grasp. In Job, chapter 28, we can read a poetic and striking expression of the sense of human ignorance, of how puny we are before the majesty and mystery of God's ways in creation. The wisdom which encompasses both intellectual insight into reality and sound judgement in life cannot (the author of Job tells us) be found by a search even as intensive as that in which men mine underground for gold and

73

precious stones. They may, indeed, succeed in that search, 'But
where shall wisdom be found? And where *is* the place of understanding? Man knoweth not the price thereof; neither is it found
in the land of the living. The depth saith, It is not in me: and the
sea saith, it is not with me. It cannot be gotten for gold, neither
shall silver be weighed for the price thereof' (vv.12–15,AV)

Today, we may be tempted to say: – Yes, indeed what else
could a second- or third-century B.C. writer say? We now know
so much more. In a year, we hear and read more variously than
most of those old Hebrew writers saw and read in a life-time. So
then, we may well ask: where is wisdom to be found and where is
the place of understanding today.

Is it to be discovered in *Private Eye*, or to be heard in 'The
World at One' or to be seen on late-night television? It does
not take one long to detect the trivialities, posturings and sheer
vacuousness of much of what we are offered today as contemporary wisdom and understanding. Perhaps we should be more
serious, and turn to sources of greater weight, for example the
intellectual enquiries that are represented (say) in various university faculties. Can any of these provide the wisdom we seek?

This is too large a theme to develop here, but I would urge that
in all the areas of human enquiry with which universities are variously engaged, ultimate questions for us are either not raised or, if
they are, are only approached: the multitudinous and variegated
studies shop short of asking them. Often this is because they
cannot be asked within the terms of reference of their particular
discourse; equally often it is not their intention to answer such
questions, even when they do arise.

Let me take one or two examples. In science, no-one asks *why*
it should be the case that the physical and biological worlds are
amenable to that kind of rational and empirical investigation
which characterize science. How does it come about that the mind
of *homo sapiens*, itself a product of evolution, can in its imagination (and one thinks of the great epoch-making leaps of human
creativity) develop such subtle models of the nature of things?
Science provides, within its own terms of reference, no explanation of why self-conscious persons should be the ultimate end-
product of the apparently fortuitous concatenation of protons,

particles and other entities, baryons, etc., which existed at the end of the first few minutes after the 'hot big-bang' of some 10,000 million years or so ago. The mystery of our presence in the universe is only heightened as we contemplate the awesome wonders of the universe we know. Remember Newton's reflections on his work – 'I do not know how I may appear to the world; but to myself I seem to have been only like a boy, playing on the sea shore, and diverting myself in now and then finding a smoother pebble, or prettier shell than ordinary, while the great ocean of truth lay all undiscovered before me!' – and that by the one whose intellectual genius still bestrides the world of science like a Colossus and who, in the *Principia*, created the greatest single work in the history of science.

But in the arts, too, the aesthetic experience, whether in the visual arts, or music, or literature, – however codified and 'compared and contrasted' (as examiners say) in its infinitely varied form and occasions – still leaves within us a questioning sense of incompleteness, a yearning for an undiscovered territory lying just out of reach of the viewer or hearer. All great art opens doors on a shining mystery, and initiates us into that which lies beyond the point of encounter between creative artist and sensitive participant.

Go and look at Rembrandt's painting of old people and his self-portraits in the National Gallery or in the Rijksmuseum in Amsterdam – look into those faces and those eyes and experience the mystery of human personality – that bottomless well into which Rembrandt penetrates and into which, not without vertigo, he lets us peer. Go and see Wagner's 'Ring' at the next opportunity and experience a sense of wonder at the unfathomable layers of meaning within the saga of dwarfs, men and gods, a mirror of the depths of the human psyche of the human condition.

So one could continue; to whichever point we turn, of the swinging compass of the studies which (we boldly say) characterise a 'univers[e]-ity', the further we proceed in any one of these directions, the greater the awe we experience of the majesty and mystery *both* of creation *and* of ourselves, who contemplate it with awe.

In Job, chapter 28, the writer concludes; 'Behold the fear of the

Lord, that is wisdom and to depart from evil is misunderstanding' (v.28). Wisdom is a spiritual quality, its origin is God himself and it is to be found only through what the writer (and other Hebrews) call the 'fear of the Lord' – that, awesome experience of the God in whom we live and move and have our being. For only as we recognise the presence of God in those intellectual, aesthetic and spiritual experiences in which we came up against the mystery and majesty of both creation and of humanity can we obtain wisdom. That, in a nutshell, is precisely what the activity of worship is about – it is about the worth-ship of God. Only in facing God for what God is can we see ourselves for what we are – and that is the beginning of wisdom. The presence of God is the place of understanding.

And now another revelation supervenes. I have already referred in various ways to the twin mysteries of the created world and of human personality existing in that created world. The essence of the Christian faith and the dynamic source of meaning in Christian worship is that these two mysteries (of the human person and of creation) have fused into one incandescent moment of unity, in the person of Jesus the Christ, which has transformed, and still does transform, our understanding of what human persons are for and what the whole creative process is about. 'The Word (of God) was made flesh and dwelt amongst us, and we beheld his glory, glory as of the only begotten of the Father, full of grace and truth'.[41] That is, God as all pervading Creator, was able at a certain time and place to manifest God's own self uniquely in and through a truly human person. In that person, the character and nature of the purpose behind creation was both consummated and unveiled. In the person of Jesus we encounter that word spoken by God in the form of a human person to enable us to know what God is like. Jesus the Christ is, as it were, in himself – in his life, death and resurrection – a living parable, in and through himself convey the truth about God who is Love.

What was unveiled, and what this means for our lives, we can gradually learn in worship, in holy communion and in lives of service. That this has happened is the core of the Gospel – so much so, that Paul could call Jesus Christ 'The power of God and the Wisdom of God'[42] and could say how much he yearned that the people of Colossi might '– come to the full wealth of conviction which understanding brings, and grasp God's secret, which is Christ himself' in whom lie hidden all the treasures of wisdom and knowledge'.[43]

Here then, in Christ is the wisdom from God – the living parable spoken by God. In the person of Christ we believe there is the clue and the place of that understanding of God's ways with humanity that makes sense of all our right and proper, but lesser, insights and enquiries – whether in art, or science or history or personal relations or society. Ultimately, this is where wisdom is to be found. May we all together learn to penetrate into that secret of Christ himself, of that human face of God, the one in whom the Word of God speaks and is embodied so that God's treasures may be revealed to us and enrich our lives.

11

One Way – or many?

Members of what is called a *uni*versity could understandably question just what the 'uni' part of the designation *'uni*versity' really amounts to. Whether it is the cornucopian variety of clubs, interests, sports or other means of using up valuable time enticingly displayed at occasions set up for Freshers, or the range of the faculty lecture lists, or of musical and other cultural events – or simply its ethnic, social and personal diversity, the individual can be simply overwhelmed by the variety of responses that is demanded.

Included in this spectrum of diversity is the responses that seems to be required from us to the range of activities associated with the word 'religion'. Etymologically it refers to what binds people together, but often the impression is of just the opposite. For, quite apart from the historical and now widely regarded as unhappy divisions within the Christian church, one hears the claims, not only of the other major world religions (Buddhism in particular these days in the West), but also the strident seductions of newcomers such as the New Age religion, Deep Ecology, Gaia-worship and even the occult (strange irruption in an educated and supposedly scientifically-based society!).

What are we to make of such a plethora of possibilities, of such a clamour of voices commanding our attention and commitment? One reaction would be to retreat into our own particular cultural and religious ghetto and to have nothing to do with anyone who thinks differently, even about the one God whom millions of different religions worship. Such seems to be the unfortunate reaction of supposed leaders of the two most extreme wings of that diverse and comprehensive body, the Church of England, to the increasing practice of having inter-faith services to articulate common concern and prayer with respect to issues that transcend the differences between the various religions (such as the need to preserve the Earth's ecology or prayer for the victims of oppression during war).

That reaction of those otherwise disparate wings of the Church is certainly one, morally, religiously and intellectually bankrupt way, of achieving a spurious peace – that of the proverbial ostrich's head buried in the sand. Another natural first reaction to the variety of forms of religion would be – 'a plague on all your houses; just leave me alone!' This would certainly simplify one's diary, but would it not mimic the ostrich just as much as the other more aggressive response? For this rich variety in what we collectively denote as 'religion' is a powerful testimony to a perennial feature of human existence which we ignore to the peril of our fullness as human beings – namely, the search for *meaning*.

This search has characterized humanity for almost as long as we have been a distinct species on the earth – certainly to a period even before 40,000 years ago, that period in which burial of human dead with ritual has been discovered amongst the Neanderthals – thereby signifying some consciousness of the ephemeral finitude of human existence and testifying to a longing for its transcendental fulfilment in another mode of existence.

It seems that human beings have indulged with extraordinary fecundity the propensity of their unique self-consciousness to search for meaning and intelligibility in the world, a search which has led them to see the world as not self-explanatory and so as created. There are good grounds for regarding such a Creator as best described as at-least-personal and to be self-communicating. So, perhaps, it is not surprising that the long search of humanity for meaning and intelligibility has not been in vain – humanity has been able to read the Creator's meanings written into his creation. The search has a long history and many have pointed to an 'axial period' around 800-200 BC, when in the three distinct and culturally disconnected areas of China, India and the West, there was, through the insights of particular individuals, a genuine expansion of human consciousness beyond that prevailing in the ancient, river-valley civilizations that had existed hitherto – the galaxy of names is staggering – Confucius, Lao-tse, the Buddha, the writers of the Upanishads, Zarathrustra, the Hebrew prophets from Elijah to the 'Second-Isaiah', Homer, Plato, Aristole, and the Greek tragedians, and so on. As Karl Jaspers has said 'What is new about this age, in all three areas of the world, is that man becomes conscious of being as a whole, of himself and his limitations ... By consciously recognising his limits he set himself the highest goals ... In this age were born the fundamental categories within which we still think today, and the beginning of the world religions, by which human beings still live, were created'.[44]

In Western civilization we stand on the road that leads from the merger of two of the trails started in this axial period in its Mediterranean focus – those of Greece and of ancient Israel, as transmitted and transmuted by two thousand years of Christian interpretation and development. We are the recipients of this double heritage – in our language, art, literature, science, ethics and institutions – and they have made us the persons we all are. We have no other resources immediately to hand whereby to articulate our search today for meaning and intelligibility. For it would take us a lifetime of immersion into the culture and languages of the Far East to get under the skin of, say, Buddhism or the religions of India in order for them really to come alive for us and to speak to us at all levels of those psyches of ours moulded by our Western heritage, sympathetic and open to their insights though we must strive to be.

When we ask the crucial question of the long serarch, 'What can we know of God's meaning for humanity?', we are compelled by our history to recognize that, unique among the formative influences in our culture, and uniquely challenging in his person and teaching, there stands the figure of Jesus of Nazareth. As Bernard Levin, who is not a Christian, somewhat surprisingly said in a knockabout article in the *Times*[45] on a projected biography of Jesus by A.N. Wilson, 'Is not the nature of Christ, in the words of the New Testament, enough to pierce to the soul anyone with a soul to be pierced? ... he still looms over the world, his message is still clear, his pity is still infinite, his consolation still effective, his words still full of glory, wisdom and love'.

So we, from within our own culture, cannot avoid asking: 'Why is Jesus of Nazareth relevant to the human search for meaning and intelligibility?' and, consequently, 'Who was/is he?' What, in the light of the most searching historical and linguistic

investigations that have been applied to that single corpus of literature we call the New Testament, can we affirm as well-founded
historically about him? At this point we have to listen carefully to
the experts. Let me tell you what I have culled from them and
their sources. First of all some historical facts, from St Paul, the
earliest of the New Testament writers:

> – Jesus existed as a human being, born of a woman (no
> mention of any virginal conception), as a member of the race
> of Israel and a descendant of David
> – he had brothers, and followers;
> – his ministry was directed towards the people of Israel;
> – he instituted the Eucharist, the Holy Communion, on the
> night that he was betrayed;
> – he was crucified;
> – he was 'raised on the third day.[46]

A similar list can be drawn from the Gospels.[47] However, these
constitute but the barest outline and need filling out with some
further historical perspectives of a more challenging nature. Some
of these are:

> – that the brief life and of this obscure Jew, Jesus, in a back-
> water of the Roman Empire, produced an effect, firstly on
> his followers and then upon the rest of the world, the magni-
> tude and quality of which demand explanation;
> – that his teachings and much in his life provided evidence
> that Jesus' relation with God was uniquely intense and inti-
> mate (e.g., his innovative use of the very personal word
> 'Abba' as a form of 'father' for addressing God in prayer) –
> he was open to God to an extent that was qualitatively
> unique;
> – that the primary stress in his teaching was the coming of
> the Kingdom of God, of the Reign of God, and that in his
> own coming and in his proclamation of the call of God to
> humanity, this Kingdom, this Reign, had been inaugurated;
> – that Jesus spoke and acted with an authority that is self-
> contradictory, inexplicable – indeed insupportable – except

on the basis of Jesus' personal identification with the
purposes of God;
– that Jesus' death was uniquely tragic, both in its implications for his message and in its manner – 'My, God, my God,
why hast thou forsaken me?' is the authentic cry from the
cross, too unexpected to be capable of invention by Mark;
– that very soon after his death, his disbanded and dispirited
followers burst onto the scene transformed by their experience of the convincing presence of Jesus in such a way that
they said he had been 'raised from the dead' – as evidenced
in their then coming together on the first day of the Jewish
week to celebrate this fact of their experiences in a meal of
bread and wine of the kind they used to share with Jesus
before his execution (what we now call Holy Communion,
the Eucharist, the Mass, the Lord's Supper). His followers
then were convinced, and the Christian church which they
started has continued in this conviction, that God took the
human Jesus through death into the life of the Godhead.

So it was that Jesus of history became the Christ of faith. The
vocabulary of the Jewish scriptures and that of the surrounding
culture were ransacked in the first century by the monotheistic,
and mostly Jewish, writers of what came to be called the *New*
Testament to find images, models and metaphors to express the
significance of the teaching, life, death and resurrection of this
completely human person through whom they had experienced
the presence and action of God himself.

Perhaps the most profound of those metaphors is to be found in
that Prologue to St John's Gospel that is, appropriately, read as the
Gospel on Christmas Day. It is the metaphor of Jesus the Christ
being the 'Word' of God ('Logos' in Greek, the 'logy' of the
names of so many nouns for our studies – geology, biology, etc. –
all words about, communication concerning, the earth, living
organisms, and so on).

I can do little justice here to the profundity of this metaphor
which this Prologue launched into our civilisation to denote that
meaning which God has all the time been expressing in and
through creation and which had now found its full expression in

the one human being who had been totally open and obedient to the purposes of God. But note that the Word of God, which both *is* God and yet distinct enough to be said to be with God, is present through the whole of creation, striving to communicate with a humanity that prefers the darkness of ignorance. It has never been absent from creation, but in Jesus we see it 'made flesh', that is the meaning of God written into creation is now expressed in a human person. What was hidden, incognito and overshadowed is now revealed, made manifest and shown as the true light of the world.

John Macquarrie has bravely attempted to write a paraphrase of the Prologue substituting for the 'Word', with a capital W, the alternative word 'Meaning', with a capital M because this 'Meaning' is closely connected with God and is virtually identical with God as the first verse of the Prologue says). The result is not – as he willingly recognises, a shining example of religious prose or verse, but it does help us to understand better what is being asserted. It includes paraphrases of those well-known verses, for example:

> 'Life is the drive towards Meaning ... Meaning shines out through the threat of absurdity, for absurdity has not overwhelmed it ... Meaning was there in the world and embodying itself in the world ... and even humanity, the bearer of Meaning, has rejected it. But those who have received it and believed in it have been enabled to become children of God ... For the Meaning has been incarnated in a human existent, in whom was grace and truth; and we have seen in him the glory towards which everything moves – the glory of God.' (*op.cit.*, n.46, pp.106-7).

In more conventional language, Jesus the Christ has revealed the nature of the self-offering, creative Love that is the God who is the source of all being.

In the introduction, I raised the question of how we are to relate to the rich variety of religions and so, implicitly, that of the uniqueness, if any, of Christian perceptions. What we can now properly affirm is that our understanding of Jesus as the manifestation of the Word, the Meaning of God expressed in creation, leaving ample room for God to have expressed his meanings to other cultures through their own resources – indeed what sort of God would it be that had *not* communicated divine meaning to the millions outside the range of the Western world? Hence we must listen to and learn from these other religions and not be disrespectful of them by thinking we can do it without immersing ourselves in their culture and languages if we are to take them seriously. Meanwhile we have good grounds for believing that in Jesus the Christ God has spoken a definitive and unique Word to humanity and expressed truly the meaning of his creation. We have the privilege of sharing with our fellow men and women of all cultures our belief that 'one who was totally and utterly a man – and had never been anything other than a man or more than a man – so completely embodied what was from the beginning the meaning and purpose of God's self-expression (… his Word …) that it could be said, and had to be said, of that man, 'He was God's man', or 'God was in Christ', or even that he *was* 'God for us'[48] – indeed true God, very God, the God who has spoken in his own distinctive ways to people of all cultures.

The Word *was* made flesh, and dwelt among us and we beheld (and behold) his glory, the glory as of the only-begotten of the Father, full of grace and truth.

The Christian Faith

12

How could Christ die 'for us'?

'The days are coming, says the Lord, when I shall establish a new covenant' with his people of Israel and Judah, Jeremiah proclaims as the message of God.[49] In it, he says, God will set his law within them, writing it in their hearts, and they really will be his people and he will be their God. But somehow, it never quite happened to the people of Israel, or to anyone else – the world seemed to go on its way much as before, a baffling mixture of good and evil, of hopes only partly fulfilled and of disillusion. Until, that is, something happened and we find a community emerging from this same people of Israel who had had an experience such that they eventually called the literature describing it 'The New Covenant', 'The New Testament' – perhaps, to use a term of pre-war American politics, we could call it 'The New Deal'. That community consisted of the followers of Jesus whom they entitled 'the Christ' – the 'Anointed One' of God.

They saw, and we have now come to see through them that, in what happened in and to Jesus, God has unmistakably shown his hand, has unveiled further the purposes he has written into the cosmos for humanity. God in and through Jesus the Christ has afforded a new definition of what it is, or rather it might be, to be and become fully human. In the resurrection of Jesus the Christ we see what kind of life it is (and the kind of death he suffered was specific to and a direct consequence of the character of his life) that can be taken up by God into the very being of God, so that death becomes the gateway into a new kind of existence. It is a life of openness to God, of oneness with God's purpose to bring his Kingdom into the life of humanity, of unstinting self-offering love of humanity through love of God.

So in Jesus the Christ we now have revealed the consummation of God's creative purposes for humanity – and the Christian tradition associates this specifically with the death and rising to life of

that same Jesus the Christ. But how can what happened in and to
him, happen in and to us? Is what happened in and to him in any
way effective in the effectual for bringing the rest of humanity
along the same 'Way'? Can it have any effects here and now,
some two thousand years later, in a way that might actually enable
us to live in harmony with God, ourselves and our fellow human
beings and so to experience the fulfilment for which human
nature yearns? The Nicene Creed speaks of Christ dying 'for us'.
What does this mean? How could Christ die 'for us'?

The possibility of answering such questions in the affirmative
can be grounded only on the fact of our sharing a common
humanity with this Jesus. Only a joint emphasis on continuity as
well as on new emergence can hope to provide any understanding
of Jesus the Christ which is going to make what he was relevant
to what we might be. For the very fact of the 'incarnation' entails
that what happened in and to Jesus is possible for all humanity
and indeed this is the basis of Christian hope. What is pivotal here
is our joint affirmation both of the continuity of the human Jesus
with the rest of creation, including humanity; and of the disconti-
nuity – the emergence in him through the divine initiative of what
is new and irreducibly distinctive in the relation of his created
human nature to God. Because of the continuities we can conjec-
ture that what happened in and to him could happen in and to us.
But because, also, it was through the fusion of his human
response and the divine initiative that Jesus of Nazareth became
the 'Christ', with all that the title has come to imply, we have to
inquire further about how the 'things about Jesus' could be operative in relation to our wills and the divine initiative, so that our
transformation into harmony with God, ourselves and our fellow
human beings becomes possible.

'God was in Christ reconciling the world to himself',[50] St Paul
attested, and the working out of how this might be so was, classi-
cally, the intention of theories of the 'atonement' (an English
word invented in the early 16th century, meaning simply: 'at-one-
ment', bringing into harmony). This is the term used to refer to
the reconciling of God and humanity – both the condition of
being 'at one' and the means whereby it is attained. But before
going further, we must take into account certain new, well-

established features of our contemporary knowledge concerning humanity.

Biological, as distinct from the spiritual, death of the individual cannot (in spite of Paul) be attributed to human 'sin', whether understood in a purely moral sense (i.e., as 'sins') or, more fundamentally, as alienation from God and humanity. For death of the individual was the divine way whereby new species were created by God through natural selection so that the death of biological individuals, incapable of sin in either sense, occurred aeons before humanity appeared on the earth. Furthermore, all the archaeological evidence points to *homo sapiens* as only gradually merging into self-consciousness with values expressed in social arrangements. Human beings never in the past had some golden age of innocence and perfection from which they have 'fallen'. Hence that story can now only be accepted as an existential insight into the perennial human condition – and a highly significant and shrewd one at that.

We need today to see how what happened to Jesus the Christ liberates us from the boundary of biological death and how it can actually effect our release from the bonds of that paradoxical state of frustrated incompleteness and alienation from God, nature and humanity which is our contemporary experience of 'original sin' – and can actually enable us to come into greater harmony with God and humanity.

So: how can what happened to Jesus the Christ all those centuries ago have significance for us there and now? Many different images and models have been used in the long history of the Church to try to understand how the life, suffering and death of Jesus the Christ, vindicated as it was by God in the resurrection, can actually effect such changes. For example, the death of Christ, in particular, has be seen variously as:

– a vicarious sacrifice;
– a demonstration of justice in which 'satisfaction' is made of the demands of justice (Anselm);
– a decisive victory over hostile evil powers (G. Aulen);
– an act of love (Abelard).

Those nurtured in the bosom of the Church and familiar, through the Old Testament, with the thought and customs of the ancient Hebrew people and other earlier times, can perhaps translate all of these images and metaphors, when they are not actually repelling, into a language meaningful for today. But it is not easy – and well nigh impossible for those outside the Church. In a way we are all outsiders in relation to the Church of the past, for too much cultural water has gone under the bridge to make a lot of its imagery readily accessible to us today. So let me try a route based on the last pointer – of atonement as an act of love.

It is essential to recall that God is One who is all the time simultaneously Creator, and Redeemer (or Liberator) and Sanctifier: God as Father, Son and Holy Spirit *is* Love.

- *Creation* is a continuing act of self-offering, self-emptying Love in which God as Father suffers in and with God's own creation, which includes humanity.
- *Redemption, (or Liberation)* is an act of re-creation of our humanity by God as Son (or Word) and release from the bondage that human alienation from God, humanity and nature involves.
- *Sanctification* is the natural uniting of ourselves with God, itself an act of continuing creation by God as Holy Spirit in human beings.

The One God in God's own ultimate Love and eternal purpose aims to create, redeem and sanctify us, to unite us with Godself.

What, then, is the significance of Jesus' suffering and cross? In Jesus, we witness a person fully open in obedience to God, so open that his human life became and continues to be the most complete expression we have of what God is like in human terms. And it was that life, a life of that kind, which led to the dereliction of his self-offering on the cross – 'for us' as the New Testament affirms and the Nicene Creed reiterates. In that life we see what God is really like, in human terms. His life is, as it were, transparent to God so that in and through him we are shown definitively the nature of God as the self-offering, vulnerable Love that goes to the uttermost to draw all humanity to him. Because of

Jesus' oneness of will with and obedience to God, he unveils what God is really like and has all the time been doing in creation. 'God suffers in the cross in *oneness* with the person of Christ; Christ suffers *eternally* in the cross; God is most *Godlike* in the suffering of the cross'.[51]

But how does what Jesus the Christ did there and then actually make us one with God here and now, twenty centuries later and release us from the bondage of our self-centredness and all that alienates us from God and each other?

What we cannot emphasize too much is that, as St Paul put it, it was *God* in Christ that was reconciling the world to God's own self . In the self-offering of the man Jesus we see God's own self suffering to draw us to him. His was the totally God-informed, God-saturated life and it was such a life that was self-offered in death for the inauguration of God's Reign, God's Kingdom among humanity – in human hearts and minds and wills. In Jesus, God broke through the barrier and simultaneously revealed both what human nature was intended to become as the true image of God; and that God is self-offering, vulnerable Love.

There were thousands of crucifixions in 1st-century Palestine, particular after the later rebellions. What was unique about that of Jesus was the nature of the life that was willingly offered, not without an immense inner struggle, and what was unique was the consequence – its vindication by God taking his whole person-hood through death into the inner life of God's own being, in fact, the resurrection.

As we contemplate the suffering and cross of Jesus Christ, we are impelled to recognize with a unique clarity and cleansing power the true nature of God as the Love that suffers for us to bring us into harmony with God's own self. In ordinary human life, the love and forgiveness of one person for another begets responsive love and repentance. As we really recognize the love of God manifest in the passion and cross of Christ, our love of God is kindled. And as God kindles this love in us, so we can be impelled to offer ourselves in love to fulfil God's purpose. Then God starts to break through our inner barriers and begins God's Rule, God's reign, in us to bring the divine creative purposes for us to their fulfilment.

Then indeed, as God is allowed gradually to take over centre after centre in ourselves, we begin gradually to be made whole, made healthy, made wholesome – which is what being saved means in the New Testament. Then does Christ begin to 'be formed'[52] in us, that is, we become more and more what we have the potential to be, namely, one with God. But it all depends on our free response to the love of God revealed in the passion and cross of Christ.

'The cup that I drink you shall drink' Jesus told his closest followers.[53] And so it still is for us here and now. We must offer our wills to God in response to the love he has revealed in Christ who suffered and died for us, so that God can, as God did in him, re-create us to become one with the God who loves us. Then, it will be true today for us that, as Paul says, in 'anyone united to Christ, there is a new creation ... a new order has already begun.' [54]

13

Jesus the Christ

the witness of Paul and the Gospels

A former Archbishop of Canterbury (Michael Ramsey) in his book on the resurrection of Christ recalls 'receiving something of a shock when it was first his privilege to attend the lectures of the late Sir Edwyn Hoskyns [at Cambridge]. The lecturer began with the declaration that as our subject was the Theology and Ethics of the New Testament we must begin with the passages about the Resurrection. It seemed to contradict all the obvious preconceptions. Was it not right to trace first the beginning of the ministry of Jesus, the events of his life and the words of his teaching? Here, surely, the essence of the Gospel might be found, and as a finale the Resurrection comes to seal and confirm the message'.[55]

He went on to say that Hoskyns was surely right, for the whole of the New Testament was written in the light of the experience of the Resurrection and that it is the true starting point for any study of it. If we were going to follow this advice, I think most of us would naturally assume that we should therefore go straightway to those passages in what we call the four Gospels where there are accounts of the experiences of the disciples on the momentous first day of the week after the crucifixion. However, we would then be as wrong as the youthful Ramsey attending his lectures in Cambridge.

For to turn first to the Gospels, as we normally see them presented at the beginning of our New Testament, would be taking no account of what we now know about the dates of their composition and the kind of documents they are. In fact, we should first go to part of the 15th chapter of St Paul's first letter to Corinthians. This is a passage whose importance cannot be exaggerated for it is our earliest and most reliable account of the Resurrection of Jesus. We can date it fairly accurately. We know from the Book of the Acts of the Apostles (chapter 18), that Paul

95

in setting up the church at Corinth was hauled by his opponents in the Jewish synagogue before the proconsul of that part of the world, Achaia. We are told in the Book of Acts that his name was Gallio and we know from an inscription found in Delphi in 1905 that this Gallio, who was the brother of Seneca, the philosopher, was proconsul in AD 51, give or take a year. Timing and mapping out Paul's travels, we find from various internal evidence that he was writing this letter back to the Corinthian church some five years after he had been there.

In this letter, Paul is reminding the Corinthians of what he had preached to them in that period around AD 51: 'I handed on to you the tradition I had received'.[56] He is at this time referring back to his own *earlier* instruction in the faith and, indeed, to his own experience on the road to Damascus. Now from other evidence we can work out that Jesus died somewhere about AD 33–5 of our calendar. Hence we can deduce that in Corinth, some sixteen to eighteen years after the event, Paul was attesting to the Resurrection on the basis of the evidence of witnesses who had instructed him about ten years earlier.

In other words, Paul is recording the experiences of witnesses not more than some six to eight years, at the most, after the event – that is why the importance of this passage cannot be exaggerated. For it tells us all that our affirmation of the Resurrection as a historical experience is well attested by witnesses close to the event. The Gospels also provide evidence, but they were written some twenty to forty years later than this letter of Paul, though undoubtedly relying on earlier documents and oral traditions now inaccessible to us.

It is necessary to emphasize that the Christian faith has genuine historical roots and that there is cogent evidence for the truth of this central affirmation of the Resurrection, and truth must always be the overriding concern of Christian and non-Christian alike. We must be concerned not with dogmatic assertion based on speaking louder than our non-believing contemporaries, but with what can be ascertained by the application of reason in the light of experience and evidence. This clearly substantiates that the early disciples of Jesus experienced the presence of this total personality as alive, as in some sense taken through death into the

presence of God. Paul simply affirms that they had this experience. The later writers of the Gospel give accounts that agree with
this broad assertion of St Paul, but vary considerably among
themselves in the details – not surprisingly if the events were so
astounding and mind-blowing as they believed. All agree that the
total person of Jesus was, in some unthinkable manner, alive in
God and to them – and notice, *en passant*, that whether or not the
tomb was empty is not central to this belief.

There was an indubitable nexus of events that transformed the
depressed and beleaguered disciples into a force that altered the
course of history and threw a flood of new light on to their understanding of Jesus' life, death and teaching. The Resurrection
enabled them to see Jesus as the Christ, the anointed of God, the
prototype of a new humanity, a new Adam, as it were – a kind
of elder in the destiny of the family of God. Paul especially
emphasises the dramatic consequences of Jesus' resurrection
for humanity – his death is understood as the end of the old
humanity symbolised by Adam and his resurrection as the burst-
ing through the cul-de-sac of death and thereby the beginning of
a new possibility for humanity. Jesus was thus a kind of new
Adam.

The Resurrection led them, as can be discerned in the Gospels
now as well as in Paul, to identify Jesus Christ with the Spirit of
God and the Wisdom of God that had been the outreach of the
transcendent God into the world in creative, providential and
redemptive concern. As Paul testifies, they found in Jesus the
climactic embodiment of that outreach, that is, they saw the
whole nexus of events surrounding him as God's own action on
behalf of humanity. In him they found the focus of the word of
God.

Notice it is Jesus the Christ who is the word of God to humanity – not the written words of the New Testament writers. They
indeed ransacked the store of images and metaphors available in
their traditions to try to express the overwhelming significance of
what they and their sources had witnessed. But their insights are
fallible and partial and have to be held in conjunction with each
other. So it is that the witness of the New Testament is pluriform
and diverse and in parts almost contradictory as the early church

faced up to the fact they had got it wrong in expecting Jesus' imminent return.

For example, we can discern a development in their use of 'Son of God' language about Jesus. For first-century Jews this was a title from the psalms for the anointed Davidic king which was already being extrapolated to apply to the Messiah, the Anointed One, whom God would send to deliver his people from religious and political oppression. Now in the earliest recoverable post-Easter proclamations and statements[57] concerning Jesus as Son of God, the most striking feature is the way this is spoken of as beginning with and from his resurrection. The mood of exhilaration that induced persists for the next fifty to sixty years, even when the emphases are different. Thus, Paul and Mark, in the earliest Gospel, seem to agree that Jesus' divine sonship was a feature of his whole ministry, especially characterized by his suffering and death. In Matthew and Luke, Jesus' divine sonship is traced back specifically to his birth and conception (Son of David by his line of descent – Son of God because of the creative power of the Holy Spirit). In the letter to the Hebrews (not by Paul), Jesus as Son of God is first seen as a thought in the mind of God that pre-exists his actual birth. Only in the Fourth Gospel ('John') does the idea emerge of Jesus as the divine Son of God from the beginning of the world and as sent into the world by the Creator-Father. So a development can be traced and any honest twentieth-century interpretation of the significance of Jesus must take into account the divergences in the earliest Christian thought as well as the convergences – not to mention the subsequent doctrinal elaborations of the Church. In doing so, however, the historic and well-founded centrality of the Resurrection remains the pivot and fulcrum of the whole process.

For overriding all else, it was the encounter of the first disciples with the living, risen Christ that was the essential core of their new life in relation to God and humanity. Later witnesses – Paul and the writers of the Gospels and other epistles – mostly had not met Jesus in the flesh but had experienced his risen presence as transforming their lives.

It can be the same for us now. We can only come to full and confident faith insofar as we put ourselves in the way of meeting the risen Christ through what have traditionally been called the 'means of grace'. That is,

> – through prayer and reflecting on what we have been shown of the nature of God and God's ways with humanity through the life, death and resurrection of Jesus the Christ;
> – through reading and thinking about the encounter with Christ of those early disciples, and their reflections on it – all of which are preserved in our New Testament;
> – through coming into the presence of Christ by receiving the sacrament of Holy Communion and by being open to the very presence, the Spirit of God, as we do so.

Then gradually we shall begin to be able to say with Paul – 'Last of all he appeared to me too'[58] and by God's grace we too shall become witnesses to the power of the God to transform human nature. It was that power which was uniquely and crucially manifest in the raising of Jesus so that we now acknowledge him as the 'Christ' – as one anointed as God's very representative in human form on earth and still present to us as the one who can raise our lives into the very presence of God.

14

The Resurrection and Human Destiny

What difference does the Resurrection, in fact, make? Does the Resurrection, does Jesus' coming at all, make any real difference to us and the world? We need to be clear what we mean by the Resurrection to which we perhaps, too glibly refer. This continues to be a subject of much serious investigation among Christian theologians and New Testament scholars. But through it all what does seem to be clear is:

Firstly, that the historical evidence is overwhelming that there was a movement of faith and insight among the early disciples of Jesus, which found expression in their earliest practices (e.g., of meeting to break bread on the first day of the Jewish week – our Sunday). This faith also found expression in their earliest preaching which undoubtedly included the proclamation that Jesus was the one whom 'God raised from the dead' – often adding 'on the third day' and 'according to the Scriptures'.

Secondly, this faith, and this insight, were triggered off by an actual nexus of events in which Jesus is descried as personally encountering his disciples (after his death) in an undoubted, authentic, and, often unexpected, manner – and Paul gives very early evidence of this.[59]

Thirdly, these triggering experiences then threw a flood of light on their understanding of Jesus' life, death and teaching, which was presented to the world in terms of the earliest announcements and its embellishments.

There has been, and still is, much debate about the relation between these three elements but it seems to me that the second – the nexus of events – is pivotal and essential. These events were of such a kind that they left no doubt in the disciples' mind that – in a way they could not fully understand, and nor we too, for that matter – the full human identity and person of Jesus had been taken through death by an act of God, so that the risen Jesus was still fully alive to them; and that this Jesus was in the very presence of God. (Although it was the Jesus they had lain in a tomb who was now, by God's act, alive to them, the question of whether or not the tomb was empty is not quite so central as some might suggest – for the means and mode of God's action may remain for ever obscure, whereas the result is well testified.)

We can now return to our earlier question and put it more bluntly: God has raised Jesus – so what? What difference does that make to ordinary human life, to lives enmeshed in work and the multitude of cares and concerns which necessarily and unavoidably are the warp and the woof of the web of life? To answer this question, we have to take a step back, as it were, from the Resurrection itself and see it in perspective by asking – *who* was raised?

'Who was raised?' Clearly it was Jesus – that is, the human being whom God took through death into His own presence was the one who in his human person expressed God's love for humanity by showing that participation in God's Kingdom was an open possibility for all willing in humility to enter it. To do this, we have to accept not the logic of prudence but to accept that the Good, that Love, is sovereign and demands absolute fidelity, of the kind shown by Jesus as he set his face to go up to Jerusalem. That Good, that Love, Jesus called 'Father' who is served only by those willing to take the risk. Whoever seeks to gain his life will lose it, and whoever loses his life in God's service will preserve it, he taught. Jesus was the one who not only said this, but actually did it – lived and died for it – and so merged his human will into the divine will that we see God uniquely acting and uniquely expressed in him.

It was then, this person so self-offered, so united with God's loving purpose, whom God 'raised'; whom God took through death into God's presence, into the divine mode of being itself. Now as we contemplate this event in this fuller perspective, we are confronted with the re-vivifying thought that the one who was raised was a human being who existed in the world as we do – made of carbon, nitrogen, oxygen and so on, as we are. His body contained all the marks of its evolutionary origins that ours do.

His DNA was patterned on the same genetic code as is ours, and as is that of all other living creatures from microbes to mammals. He, too, like us, represented an apparently temporary configuration of the stuff of the world – but a configuration which thinks, loves and knows itself, as we do.

In himself, he represented, as a human being like us, the fundamental mystery, glory and tragedy of the cosmos. The mystery is that a personal creature like ourselves should have emerged at all out of the non-living world – so that in us the stuff of the world becomes persons, with mental and spiritual lives and activities and embodying values – those qualities which constitute our peculiar glory, and the peculiar tragedy of our eventual death. Glory because in humanity we see the potentialities of the cosmos being actualised in our self-conscious existence; tragedy because we who have emerged from the matrix of nature are aware of our as yet unfulfilled potentialities. We strive to become what we are not yet; we have ideals and purposes which we unsuccessfully seek to embody in social structures and created forms. But always we are frustrated by two apparently insurmountable obstacles: by our ignorance of what we should become and by death.

All non-human creatures simply react to changes in the environment made by causes beyond their control. But we alter our environment, in malice or benevolence or in sheer ignorance, and thus shape ourselves and our future. We alone choose between ends and are faced with the question: What should I, what should we, be striving to become? Human culture records many ideals which have moved humanity: some noble, as the Platonic; some amiable, as the English gentleman; some austere, as the Stoic; some trivial, as in the modern cult of pop-singers.

Is this then what Christ must be for the world? An ideal set before us all? Certainly he is at least that to many, and we must be grateful for it. But in itself it is a distorting dilution of that great affirmation of the early Church that God having expressed Godself in creation (we would say today by eliciting persons out of insentient inorganic matter) 'has in this final age ... spoken to us in the Son whom he has made heir to the whole universe, and through whom he created all orders of existence.'[60]

In the light of this, in the perspectives and language of our own times, we can now say that the evolutionary process through which God has hitherto chosen to express his creative power was lifted on to an entirely new level when God expressed himself in and through the humanity of Jesus the Christ. Christ is, in this sense, the summit of evolution. When, on the cross, he said 'It is finished,' it was the whole costly, creative, loving purpose of God which was consummated.

In Jesus, we see a new kind of human life which God all along intended that human beings should have in harmony with God's creative purposes. Jesus the Christ himself represented human perfection not in its particular, but in its most universal form. His was a human life which was itself a perfect creation expressing the fundamental elements of perfected humanity. Christ was not the perfect artist, or composer, or scientist, or statesman. This would have been a restriction and limitation. His humanity is universal because it is potentially what all of us have in our nature to become. Christ is the universal human being – in the mythology, the 'second Adam' – because he is the fulfilment of those potentialities which all possess.

Throughout the long aeons of biological evolution, the death of the individual has been the necessary means for new forms of life to emerge in succeeding populations. But in *homo sapiens* the individual of the species becomes aware of his or her own finitude and is affronted by it – we cannot contemplate it with equanimity. *Homo sapiens* early developed burial rituals and it is a mark of the species, distinguishing it from the higher primates, for example. Yet death is biologically inevitable and the dispersal of all our atomic and molecular components, which have been the matrix of our mental and spiritual activities, is certain for each of us. Is this then what the cosmos leads up to in its most glorious manifestation – to end not with a bang, but a whimper? a tale told by an idiot signifying nothing?

This is what I would have to conclude but for the Resurrection of Jesus. For we have seen that Jesus was all that God intends humanity to be, that in him the creative purpose of the cosmos was consummated. In him God unmistakably showed his hand; for he alone of all human beings risked all for his conviction that Love is sovereign – and God vindicated him by taking him through death. Thereby he showed unmistakably that Love conquers all.

Without this act of God in raising Jesus, we might have worked out for ourselves that there was a purpose of love shaping the cosmos – but always our failure to actualise our potential and the fact of death would have dragged us down again. But *God raised Jesus* and thereby vindicated, sealed and blessed his life, that life which risked all for Love. This assurance does now make all the difference. For this to have happened is already to have released new life-bearing forces into the world, however much the landscape of our lives may appear unchanged.

So, we ask again what does it mean for us in our ordinary lives now? It means this. We have seen that the development of our own individual abilities and potentialities may be properly regarded as the fulfilment of God's creative purposes, as this development occurs within the larger re-shaping of our lives which is the following of Jesus the Christ, and all that that implies. What we are assured of now, by Jesus' Resurrection, is that our real, actual humanity is capable of being taken by God into His presence. Every skill and facet of ourselves that has been developed within an intention to serve God and Him alone (and without regard to self) can be taken up into God. Nothing of the good, the beautiful, the true, the loving, the serving, the selfless, the creative in our ordinary lives will be lost – for God acts to draw all these into His own ultimate Being. Death has in Christ been transformed into the means whereby God lovingly takes into God's own eternal Being, all-that-we-have-become in our lives, all that which is according to God's purposes of creative love – and purges us of that which is not so in accord. Indeed 'purge' is the wrong word, for all else turns out to be simply – nothing. Let St Paul have the last word: 'God ... ordained' that we should 'share the likeness of his Son, so that he might be the eldest among a large family ... and those whom he called he also justified, and those whom he justified he also glorified.'[61]

15

Going up?

On the Mount of Olives outside Jerusalem, there is a small mosque, a former Crusader octagonal church. Inside enthusiastic guides point out to the faithful, if gullible, pilgrims a large rock on whose upper surface there is an impression which, they will be told, is a footprint left in the rock when Jesus become skyborne at his Ascension! Certainly, Luke in his Gospel said that 'While he [Jesus] was blessing them, he withdrew from them and was carried up into heaven'.[62] But 'heaven,' the more sophisticated reader would have known, is a common Jewish synonym for 'the presence of God' or just 'God'. So the disciples, we are being told, knew that Jesus was from then on in the very presence of God and would not be experienced by them again in the same way as hitherto. From this narrative of the Ascension his followers have inferred that the humanity of Jesus the Christ now dwells within the very life of the Godhead and is glorified and perfected.

This affirms that our full humanity, our maturity as human beings, is to be measured by nothing less than what Jesus the Christ is and became – a human being capable of being taken up into the life of the Godhead.

But, we may well ask, is that also *our* destiny? Are we, do we want to be, going in that direction? So reflection on the Ascension raises a whole host of questions: What are we? Where are we going? And so, where do we come from? Are we, as some Victorians argued about so vehemently after Darwin, fallen angels or rising beasts?

The image of human beings as now existing as a kind of fallen angel, creatures who have lost the primal innocence and beauty they once possessed in a golden age of Paradise, had become firmly entrenched in Christendom – and especially among our forbears in this island through the powerful influence of Milton's great, and today much neglected, words of *Paradise Lost* and

Paradise Regained. This picture was rudely shattered when Darwin produced the first evidence that *homo sapiens* has descended by natural means from more modest, and less august, origins than the perfect humanity of a primal Adam – hence the revised image of human beings as rising beasts rather than fallen angels. Darwin was right to the extent that the evidence today is overwhelming that human beings have emerged gradually *into* consciousness, self-consciousness, self-transcendence and so, concomitantly, have become capable of choice – and so of moral failure, of acting against God's will and purposes for them.

Accepting that new knowledge, as we must, Christians can no longer now be expected to see the significance of the work of Christ for the nature and destiny of humanity as simply a reversal of a past, supposed, historic 'Fall' from grace. Rather, the effect of Christ on humanity has to be seen as the actualisation of a potential, the fulfilment of a hope; it is precisely here that the Ascension is so significant – an event too much underplayed in the Western Church and rightly emphasised in the Eastern.

Admittedly there have been crude representations of this last definitive experience of the disciples of the risen Christ, not least in the visual arts with the depiction of the disciples looking up at the soles of Jesus' feet disappearing into a cloud! The New Testament writers were not really so naïve, for the same Luke, who describes the disciples' experience of the Ascension in the terms I mentioned, goes on later to put into Paul's mouth the recognition that 'the God who created the world ... is not far from each one of us, for in him we live and move and in him we exist'. And later writers were quite well aware that in no sense was God physically 'up'. As Origen said, two centuries later: 'We must interpret those passages [of Scripture] which if taken literally, are thought by the simple to assert that God is in a place, in conformity with large and spiritual ideas about God'.[63]

So is it all just a mistake to talk about 'Ascension'? That it has nothing to do with going up at all? If we were to say so, we would be just as wrong as with a literalist understanding. For, supremely, the Ascension is all about directions, about ends, about our destiny – let us try to see why.

In the New Testament, there is an intimate and close relation,

often indeed coincidence, between the experiences of the risen
Christ, including the Ascension, and the first experiences of God
as Holy Spirit – even though Luke, but not John, spreads them out
symbolically over the classical 40 days of Hebrew tradition
(hence the separation between Easter and Whitsunday even today
in our calendar). What is quite clear from the New Testament is
that:

●   The total human personhood of Jesus, which had been taken
    through death, had been revealed as having been exalted into
    the very presence of God – symbolised by the 'cloud' of the
    glory of the presence of God (Shekinah).
●   That this revelation of the exaltation of Jesus the Christ (as
    they now called him) into the life of the Godhead implied a
    new kind of way in which that Christ was to be present to all
    humanity.

The Word-of-God-made-flesh is now known to be present to us
by being released, as it were, deep within the psyches of those
whose centre is these events in which the love of God for us has
been unequivocally revealed. Thereby the image of God can be
created in us and we can become what God intends us to be. St
Paul[64] calls it Christ being 'formed in' us and the letter to the
Ephesians sees the goal of our existence as to 'come to the unity
of the faith and of the knowledge of the Son of God, to maturity,
to the measure of the fall stature of Christ'.[65]

That outreach of God to humanity that is God as Holy Spirit, is
now active to bring human beings to their full potentiality as
children of God whose destiny is to rise into the very life of God.
As William Temple once put it, 'The ascension of Christ is his
liberation from all restrictions of time and space. It does not
represent his removal from earth, but his constant presence
everywhere on earth ... now he is united with God, he is present
wherever God is present; and that is everywhere. Because he is in
heaven, he is everywhere on earth; because he is ascended, he is
here now. In the person of the Holy Spirit he dwells in his Church,
and issues forth from the deepest depths of the souls of his
disciples, to bear witness to his sovereighty'.[66] At the Ascension

it is the Word-made-flesh that enters the Kingdom of God. Jesus takes there with him his human nature and opens the gates of the Kingdom of God to humanity.

It was our humanity that in Jesus the Christ was taken up into the Godhead and is still there. That is why the 'Ascension of Christ to the Father', as it is sometimes expressed, represents the fulfilment and consummation of the cosmic creative process which brought into existence creatures, ourselves, destined through our free response to share in the life of God our Creator. Because –

> through the Ascension we now know it has happened to Jesus the Christ, we know it can happen to us too if we are open to God as Holy Spirit, to reshape our human existence, inner and outer, into that transformed humanity of which Jesus is the paragon, paradigm, archetype and supreme revelation.

Because –

> of his Ascension we can now have the hope of becoming what God intends us to be.

Because –

> Jesus the Christ is risen and ascended, humanity is now know to have as its destiny entry into the very life of God, for he was and is the pioneer of our salvation[67] – he blazed the trail to the fulfilment and consummation of what God intends for humanity.

So we can know that our own, individual, deeply personal, development can, in spite of all, have a direction – it is towards God. Christ became what we are, in order that we might become as he is now, with God. So, after all, our direction, pioneered by Christ, can indeed be up! So we really can pray, in the words of the Collect for Ascension Day:

'Grant, we beseech thee, Almighty God, that like as we do

believe thy only-begotten Son our Lord Jesus Christ to have ascended in to the heavens; so we may also in heart and mind thither ascend, and with him continually dwell, who is alive and reigns with thee and the Holy Spirit, one God, world without end.'

immanent. It is the one God at work in the one process — for us, for our fruition into God.

The wonder is that, when we allow ourselves to become part of this healing, healthy process initiated by God, we become more, not less, open to the presence of God in the created world and in the creative works of humanity. We then come to see that the intended destiny for the spirit of humanity is unity with the Spirit of God, as that inner light which is our birthright is united with the Uncreated Light that illumines all creation and creativity; as the small spark of the potential divinity within us is fanned into coalescence with the tongues of the bright flame of the very Presence of God — the fire of the divine Presence that descended on that first day of Pentecost long ago and is still with us here and now.

> 'The dove descending breaks the air
> With flame of incandescent terror
> Of which the tongues declare
> The one discharge from sin and error.
> The only hope, or else despair
>   Lies in the choice of pyre or pyre—
>   To be redeemed from fire by fire.
> Who then devised the torment? Love.
> Love is the unfamiliar Name
> Behind the hand that wove
> The intolerable shirt of flame
> Which human power cannot remove.
>   We only live, only suspire
> Consumed by either fire or fire.'
>   (T. S. Eliot, *Little Gidding* IV)

In the Name of the Father and of the Son and of the Holy Spirit

In nomine Domini, Patris, Filii et Spiritu Sancti

It is these words that the Vice-Chancellor admits members of Oxford University to the degree of M.A. – a curious fact which, from time to time, arouses opposition among some students and senior members and would no doubt excite more were it not decently obscure in the words of a dead language! Some react with disdain, cynicism, even; others with indifference; yet others with some piety as the time-honoured phrase is recited over bowed heads. In any case, few, or none, fail to acquiesce! It is not my purpose now to justify this odd survival – though it can scarcely be considered inappropriate in a university which incorporates a prayer for divine enlightenment in its crest. My purpose is, rather, to direct your attention to this odd phrase itself – 'In the Name of the Father, and of the Son and of the Holy Spirit'.

With these words Christians are baptised, with these words they give the ring in marriage, in this Name they pray and are dismissed from the Holy Communion, in this Name the last rites are performed. Yet the more one thinks about it the odder the phrase appears – one 'Name', yet attributed to three in the words that follow.

To the Biblical writers and the ancient world the name of thing, and especially of a person, was more than a mere label, for it expressed the distinctive character and inner being of the person. So the first assertion of the phrase is the primary conviction that God is one. Standing where we are within a culture saturated with half-forgotten Christian terminology, we too readily relapse into a confused tri-theism, forgetting that the oneness of God is the basic pre-supposition of Christian thought and practice.

If there is anything for which humanity is indebted to the

people of Israel, it is for their preserving and enriching their primal insight at Mount Sinai into the transcendent power of the one God who is over all – whom they came to speak of as Creator, invisible, without gender, universal, over all people, in all places and who required righteousness. This conviction was not the result of philosophical reflection but was hammered out in their history, through exile, suppression, and martyrdom and had to be recognised even by the might of Rome. Every morning and evening the faithful Jew recited, and still does, the Shema beginning: 'Here O Israel, the Lord our God is one Lord'.[72]

It was as a child of Israel that Jesus came and it was, amazingly, men and women of Israel, whose distinctive existence was involved in their belief in the oneness of God, who were first impelled to recognise in Jesus a nature which possessed a more-than-human, divine dimension.

We recall: Peter's 'You are the Christ' – that is, the Anointed One, God's son, long-awaited by Israel; Thomas's 'My Lord and my God'.

What was it that impelled devout monotheistic Jews to say such things of Jesus, the carpenter of Nazareth? There was his impelling personality; there was his authority over human beings, over disease; there was his dynamic power which they saw as the breaking-in of God's Kingdom into history in Jesus' own presence among them; there was the conviction that the Way which he trod was the only way open to those who seek both truth and fullness of life. It was, above all, the power of his Resurrection which finally so impelled them. That which produced such a radical revision of the thinking of devout men of Israel must have had the character of a unique disclosure of God.

But this was not and is not all. For God to be known as transcendent Creator, the Father of all, and to have come once in history as Mediator between God and humanity would scarcely be good news for the healing of men and nations if it remained a past event, gone for ever. It could only create in us the deepest despondency – were it not that the first disciples discovered that God himself was at work within the inner life of each one of them. This presence of the go-between God was experienced as personal – an indwelling Presence. Thus it was that the earliest

Christians came to recognise that the one God, whose oneness they continued unwaveringly to affirm, had disclosed himself to humanity as Father-Creator; as Jesus the Christ, the self-expression of God in human form; and as the Holy Spirit of God within, the Lord and Giver of life.

Do not be misled by the use of the word 'person' in this context. When we refer to the 'three persons' of the Triune God, we do not mean three individual centres of consciousness (the usual modern sense of the word), but rather the three masks of God, somewhat as in a play when we list the *dramatis personae*. Thus the unity of God is not a merely negative assertion – that God is not many – but that God is now revealed and experienced as comprehending within the divine being a rich diversity-in-unity – a unique integrated Unity far surpassing that of all else. The unity of God's being is not an arithmetical property, for His Being is a unity of diverse modes – more like that of a great work of art, or of a living organism, or, perhaps most of all, that of a truly integrated human person.

We are bound to ask is there *one* word, *one* name, to express this unity of the Godhead? The first Epistle of John gives the answer direct: 'God is *Love*.'[73] Love is the unifying power which, between people, expresses itself through the self-offering of one person for another.

The three-fold nature of the one God who is Love is experienced by most Christians not at the level of the intellectual stratosphere of doctrinal statements but in prayer. I am not talking here of some 'contemplative' elite, but of anyone who regularly spends even a very short time in a quiet waiting upon God. Often what is encountered is darkness, obscurity, and distraction – the relationship is one unlike any other – one that relates those who pray to that without which they would not be in being at all – a relation of absolute dependence.

But, amid this obscurity, it usually dawns bit by bit on the person praying that this activity of praying, which at first seems all one's own doing, is actually the activity of another. It is the experience of being 'prayed-in'. Recall St Paul: '... the Spirit helps us in our weakness; for we do not know how to pray as we ought, but that very Spirit intercedes with sighs too deep for words'.[74] We are caught up, as it were, in a divine conversation, passing back and forth in and though the one who prays. As we pray, God as Holy Spirit within us, God-within-us, speaks to God who is over all and transcends us. Through God as Holy Spirit we pray to God as Father. God as Holy Spirit is 'here the current of divine response to divine self-gift in which the one who prays is caught up and thereby transformed.'[75] It is from this experience of God as Holy Spirit within us, moving us to approach God as Father that we go on to appreciate the true mystery and richness of God as Son – 'no one can say 'Jesus is Lord' except by the Holy Spirit'.[76]

For when Christians pray like this, their experience of participation in a divine dialogue is an experience of God-with-us, for the one who prays begins to glimpse what it might mean to be 'in Christ'. It is to allow oneself to be shaped by prayer by the mutual interaction between the God-in-us (God as Holy Spirit) and the God-to-us (God as Father), so that we make the transition from simply regarding Christ as an external model for imitation to entering into the essence of what Christ was and is – the life of God's own self-in-humanity, our humanity. 'It is no longer I who live, but it is Christ who lives in me.'[77] In such prayer the activity of God re-models us to become 'other Christs' in the particularly of our own lives – and perhaps even do 'greater works'.[78]

This means that, as in the life of the historical Jesus of Nazareth, Jesus the Christ, the God whom Christians meet in such prayer is also one who appears for very long periods to desert us, or even to press upon us negatively causing deep disturbance and uneasiness – the death throes of the domineering ego. But through suffering comes glorification[79] – what appears to be divine absence is later seen in actuality as a grace of divine hiddenness. For through such prayer and such experiences God acts in us to make us whole, conscious and unconscious, integrating all our levels of being – even the dark ones we prefer to repress. In such prayer God also acts to make us whole together – that is what the Paul's language about being 'in Christ' means. We share together this experience of the oneness of our relation to God as Father, through God as Son, and in God as Holy Spirit.

Thus it is that we come to experience that ultimate unity whose name is Love – that Name of Love which, as F. D. Maurice put it 'is a Name which is implied in our thoughts, acts, words, in our fellowship with each other; without which we cannot explain the utterances of the poorest peasant, or of the greatest sage; which makes thoughts real, prayers possible; which brings distinctness out of vagueness, unity out of division; which shows us how, in fate, and not merely in imagination, the love of God may find its reflex and expression in the love of man, and the love of man its substance, as well as its fruition, in the love of God'.[80]

So we pray
  'to God as Father'
    'through God as Son'
      'in God as Holy Spirit' –
In the Name of the Father and of the Son and of the Holy Spirit –
  In nomine Domini, Patris, Filii et Spiritu Sancti.

The Christian 'Way'

18

The Vision of Greatness

We hear constantly from advertisements and the media of our supposed need to fulfil our potential – we are offered various kinds of courses in developing our self-confidence, memory, self-defence, self-assertiveness and so forth. They play on our presumed dissatisfaction with our looks, age, job, and general image, which, apparently, includes what car we drive and what drinks we consume. They purport to offer something better than the state we think we're in and exploit the common feeling many of us have that we are not getting anywhere very fast!

The proffered palliatives for this state are undoubtedly false and meretricious, but the problem to which they address themselves is a genuine one:– What are we becoming? What should we be becoming? Where are we going? Even – what are we for? To ask such questions is a peculiarly human phenomenon. All other living creatures have evolved to be adapted to their environments, with limited memories and anticipation of their futures so that if the biological needs of food, sex and shelter are met they live and procreate happily enough – few, or none, commit suicide individually.

But not so with human beings, who suffer from a congenital dis-ease, a lack of satisfaction with their situation even when all their biological needs are met. As Thomas Chalmers, the great Presbyterian preacher of the last century put it:

'There is in man, a restlessness of ambition; an interminable longing after nobler and higher things, which nought but immortality and the greatness of immortality can satiate; a dissatisfaction with the present, which never is appeased by all that the world has to offer; an impatience and distaste with the felt littleness of all that he finds, an unsated appetency for something larger and better, which he fancies in the perspective before him – to all of which there is nothing like among any of the inferior animals, with whom there is a certain squareness of adjustment ... between each desire and its corresponding gratification ... No so with man ... '[81]

What, then, is that elusive, unknown state for which we yearn, if only unconsciously? What should we be becoming?

This need for an ideal manifests itself in many bizarre ways in our society's adulation of sporting figures, pop stars and operatic tenors. But many, indeed most, of these idols prove to have feet of clay – as we have seen boxing champions, leading politicians and electronic evangelists show down in flames by the same tabloid press that raised them up in the first place. So to where should we turn for our ideals of human being? This is still far from being a trivial question and lies at the heart of our confusions concerning education.

Education continues through the whole of life from the first glimmerings of our consciousness, and perhaps even before that, to the last. In what direction should we look for our ideals in this lifelong process? What is the point on the horizon to which we should steer the ship of our lives? I am reminded of the remark of Sir Richard Livingstone, classicist, a President of St John's College, Oxford, and a great educator, that 'It is right to teach the pupil to criticize but it is even more important to train them concurrently to admire ... Nothing – not all the knowledge in the world – educates like the vision of greatness and nothing can take its place.'

It is the vision of greatness that educates, for to educate is, as the Latin origin of the word shows, to 'lead out' – to lead towards a goal and a vision. It is the vision of greatness that can lead out humanity and which humanity seeks, even misguidedly through trivia and false idols. I recall as an adolescent reading biographies of Newton, Rembrandt and Beethoven and I remember, even now quite vividly, the experience of a sudden expansion of my horizons as I caught a glimpse of what human genius in science, art and music can be – and this constituted a turning point in my own education. As so it must have been for many of us – we glimpse through the garden gate vistas of a landscape richly endowed, awaiting exploration.

But, most will say, and I certainly had to recognize it, we are not going to be geniuses in science, art, music or whatever. We are quite ordinary people of only modest endowments. We have to ask what is a possible ideal for us?

The people of Israel certainly had such a vision of greatness for ordinary people – it is one of their richest gifts to civilization. We recall the traditional voice of Moses which was, and still is, the core of Hebrew education,

> 'Therefore shall ye lay up these words in your heart and in your soul ... And you shall teach them your children, speaking of them when thou sittest in thine house, and when thou walkest by the way, when thou liest down, and when thou risest up'[82]

and the even more famous exhortation from the prophet Micah:

> 'He hath shewed thee, O man, what is good; and what doth the Lord require of thee, but to do justly, to love mercy, and to walk humbly with thy God'.[83]

It was this that nurtured Jesus of Nazareth as he grew up. Is it here in Jesus that Christians should identify the supreme embodiment of that greatness which is to be the inspiration of education? Yes, indeed, I *do* want to say that, but we have to ask carefully in what respect are we to be inspired by Jesus of Nazareth.

For he was not a great scientist, artist, musician, writer – or great in any of the other spheres of human life to which the word 'genius' usually applies. He was certainly very intelligent, skilled in pungent narrative and in pithy, often ironic, parables and exceptional in his effects on his contemporaries and in his personal relations – not least in his positive and open treatment of women, children and other second-class citizens of his times. He was certainly a devoted follower of those commandments I've just summarized and he called his fellow Jews to be faithful to them.

However, his distinctiveness does not lie in this – there were prophets before and noble rabbis after him who did and said as

much. What is distinctive about Jesus is that he constituted the
consummation of human evolution, and indeed of human genius,
in his openness to God and in the obedience of his genuine human
will to God. And that is something of which we are all in
principle capable, regardless of our skills, social background
and genetic endowment. It is, to use his words, the 'one thing
needful', the 'treasure buried in the field', worth more than
anything else, the 'pearl of great price' for which we should give
our all. It is indeed the Reign of God in us, the Kingdom of God
which begins within us, the minute seed that produces fecund
growth.

For all of us – brilliant or stupid, well-off or deprived, male or
female, young or old – all of us are capable of opening our hearts
and minds and souls to God so that God becomes the centre of our
existence and not our own petty selves. Then we might also come
to see other people who are equally God's concern become ours
too, so that we forget ourselves in the joint love of God and love
of neighbour.

In Jesus the Christ, we encounter the apogee of humanity, a
humanity as-it-were saturated with the presence of God. What the
Christian Gospel is about is, to put it bluntly, that what happened
in Jesus can begin to happen in us. For alone among the objects of
human idealism, Jesus the Christ is also the *means* whereby the
ideal we see in him can actually be made reality in us.

As we respond to the presence of God in him, we come to experience God acting in him and we see that God is self-offering,
vulnerable but creative Love – and that response can begin
slowly, so slowly but so surely, to transform us – gently turning
the prow of the ship of our life towards that ultimate harbour
which is union with God. The only act of will needed on our part
is the one in which we accept that we need God to take the rudder
of our lives. Or, to change the metaphor, like St Paul, we need to
run in our lives with our eyes set on the finishing line –

'It is not that I have already achieved this. I have not yet
reached perfection, but I press on, hoping to take hold of that
for which Christ once took hold of me. My friends, I do not
claim to have hold of it yet. What I do say is this: forgetting

what is behind and straining towards what lies ahead, I press towards the finishing line, to win the heavenly prize to which God has called me in Christ Jesus.'[84]

This is the vision, transcending any merely human greatness, which constitutes the true education, the true 'leading out', of us all and, uniquely among the noblest of human ideals, it has the power of effecting in us that after which we strive. For in Jesus the Christ, we encounter the love of God fully operative in a human life and, if we follow him, that same God works within our own spirit to unite us with himself both here and now – and there and then in that eternity beyond space and time to which we will, in the end, all come.

19

Stir up!

The collect for the last Sunday of the Church's year, the Sunday next before Advent, is one of the most famous of the jewels in that crown of the English language constituted by the collects of the Book of Common Prayer:

> 'Stir up, we beseech thee, O Lord, the wills of thy faithful people; that they, plenteously bringing forth the fruit of good works, may of thee be plenteously rewarded; through Jesus Christ, our Lord. Amen'.

The set readings in Advent often speak of waiting with alertness and watchfulness: '... for you do not know when the master of the house will come ... what I say to you and I say to all: Keep awake.'[85]

Such calls to wakefulness and continued activity only too readily fall on deaf ears. We find the author John of the last book of our New Testament, the Revelation, discharging broadsides at some of the churches of Asia Minor who amongst other things, 'had lost their first love'; or had followed false teachings; or had become 'lukewarm, neither hot nor cold'. There are may snags and snares awaiting those who day in and day out attempt to follow the call to Christ over their whole lifetimes.

We can readily become insensitive, complacent and lukewarm. Or we can become so sensitive to our situation that we fall into despair – as did Elijah who, when fleeing from the wrath of Jezebel, cried to God to take away his life. But, the story in the first Book of Kings continues, he was fed and found his way to that very mountain where Moses had so encountered the living God that the life and destiny of the whole people of Israel had been transformed. And there Elijah too has an experience of the presence of God – not in the wind, or the earthquake, or in the fire, but in a still small voice that ordered him to go back through the dreaded desert to his people and to start the process of re-establishing its kingly and prophetic succession. This dramatic story reminds us that the stirring up of our wills does not occur through external forces but in being quite and alert, so that we can actually hear the 'still, small voice' of God guiding us to do what is against our natural self-protective wishes.

But the call to stir up our wills still comes to us here and now today. What can it possibly mean in our context? However concerned we may or may not be with those in other places, God's call is to us here and now, in a university as students of the things of the mind, of human culture, of the natural world. And we too can respond with either complacency or despair.

We can indeed simply ignore the whole intellectual and cultural scene and pretend that, because we are Christians, we are somehow protected from the winds that blow, and so retreat complacently into backward-looking forms of the Christian faith that simply rest upon past authorities and ignore its actual present intellectual situation.

But that is *not* how we learned Christ; it is not what he himself did in his own day as he opened the hearts of men and women to the challenge of entering the Kingdom, the Reign, of God, as he gave them a drink of new wine that could not be contained in old bottles. It was not what St Paul did as he shaped his understanding of the presence of God in Christ for the Gentile world. It was not what the Christian church did in the first few centuries of its existence when it became the faith that now reaches us nearly two millennia later and when it not only out-lived but also out-thought its pagan rivals in philosophy and religion. It is not what Thomas Aquinas did when the science and philosophy of Aristotle descended like a thunderbolt on the seminaries of the West during the thirteenth century through the intermediary of the Arab world.

Thus, if in our complacency we simply refer back to what is now our past, we fail to respond to the challenges of our times in the way that Jesus, and those who have most closely followed him, did in their day – by being open to the future and prepared to grapple with the challenges to the Kingdom of God which come from all rival views of nature, humanity and God in our own culture. Alternatively, faced by the present intellectual scene we may be tempted to succumb to despair. Sometimes the attacks on the Christian faith seem to be so numerous and forceful that we are tempted to lose heart. Yet, often in the past, it was but a very small, creative minority that rose to the challenge of their times.

I cannot help recalling accounts of that great procession which was held to celebrate the ending of the First World War. The long procession of glittering military splendour, with all its plumes and shining armour and swirling kilts and rousing music, wended its way past the throngs that filled the streets of London to their grateful cheers and plaudits, only to be followed by an anti-climax – a motley and shuffling group of older men and some women, in ordinary raincoats not marching in any good order, for some were limping. As they passed a puzzled silence would fall upon the crowd – until that is, the murmur spread that these were actually the Old Contemptibles, the small band who had crossed the Channel and held up the might of the Kaiser's army's against all odds in those first days of jeopardy in 1914.

So might the first Apostles appear to us, bringing up at the rear the tail-end of any splendid procession of the great figures of the church – a very small band to have changed the face of history.

Hence there is no need for despair on account simply of numbers. Moreover, the Christian faith is not alone in being the target of scepticism, or even cynicism. For, surveys of the cultural scene show that the intellectual climate of these last decades of our century is unprecedentedly volatile. For there is hardly a university discipline which is not questioning its own assumptions and wondering what kind of wisdom it is actually giving to the world, either in thought or in practical applications. In fact, Christianity in its central affirmations (if not in its secondary, popular beliefs) has been far less damaged than many would have thought possible in the middle decades of the century. Certainly, in our society, both Marxism and optimistic humanism, which many thought to be the chief candidates to replace it, have faded far more notably that the following of Christ and belief in God. Professor Keith Ward, now the Regius Professor of Divinity of Oxford University, a few years ago in a series of BBC programmes, in which he interviewed creative thinkers and scientists over a wide range of disciplines, could point[86] to a turning of the intellectual tide in favour of the affirmation of the transcendent in its Christian form – little though this is understood by the media in general.

Furthermore in the perplexities of our times, which do not grow any the less, Christianity is proving to have hidden resources of resilience in times of crisis, for it has always recognized the human power for evil as well as for goodness – it was at home in the catacombs and in exile, long before it was at home in the great civilization it helped to build. Thus, in our present situation as Christians in an intellectual community, we must eschew both complacency and despair. But what are we to do, to respond to the call to 'stir up our wills'?

I suggest at least one aim that those of us who are students, researchers or scholars could adopt in our present situation. We all individually are studying some major aspects of the fruits of the human mind and culture, some area of knowledge of humanity and/or nature. I suggest that it is a duty laid upon us as Christians to think through all that our particular sphere of human knowledge implies for the Christian understanding of the world and of humanity within it as we have received it from the past.

As with Elijah, it may well be that we will have to go back to that wilderness in which our faith in God – as Father, Son and Holy Spirit – may hang on a thread. But this we must be prepared to face; and God will feed us even in such a despair. For unless we strive to out-think the spurious claimed substitutes for the Christian faith, the yearning mass of our contemporaries will never even hear what God in Christ is seeking through the Holy Spirit to tell them.

That, in a nutshell, seems to me to be a call addressed uniquely and specifically to Christians who are privileged with higher education. If we fail in this, there is no-one else to take our place.

20

'Not disobedient to the heavenly vision'

Perhaps the most notable throw-away line in a scientific paper occurred in the April 25th, 1953, issue of the journal *Nature* when, in a brief note, James Watson and Francis Crick described for the first time the molecular structure of deoxyribonucleic acid, DNA. Having outlined their proposed structure, they remarked – almost in an aside – 'It has not escaped our notice that the specific pairing we have postulated immediately suggests a possible copying mechanism for the genetic material'. 'It has not escaped our notice ...' – it certainly hadn't! Nor did it escape anyone else's, and that paper became the ignition point of that explosion we call molecular biology and the whole modern movement in biology, the Genome Project, 'genetic engineering' to cure inherited disease and much else.

There is a parallel throw-away line in the history of Christianity and its consequences we have an even better chance to perceive over nineteen centuries later. In the 26th chapter of the Acts of the Apostles we read Luke's account of Paul's defence before King Agrippa. He described, very much in line with the other narrative accounts in the same book of the Acts of the Apostles, his experience on the Damascus road. He recalled how, about midday, he heard a voice and had seen a light 'from heaven' – and the voice, he said, was that of Jesus who told him that he, Saul (as he then was), in persecuting those who were following the Way of Jesus, was persecuting Jesus himself. In the vision, Jesus gave him orders to go to Damascus and commissioned him to be the apostle to the Gentiles. Then, with an uncharacteristic, almost Anglo-Saxon understatement, Paul pauses in his story and turns to his royal listener remarking, 'Wherefore, O King Agrippa, I was not disobedient to the heavenly vision'. 'Not disobedient'! – this is

137

the one who, some decade and a half later, reluctantly recounts some of his subsequent experiences to Corinthians who had doubted his authenticity:

> 'Five times I have received at the hand of the Jews the forty lashes less one. Three times I have been beaten with rods; once I was stoned. Three times I have been shipwrecked; a night and a day I have been left adrift at sea; on frequent journeys, in danger from rivers, danger from robbers, danger from my own people, danger from Gentiles, danger in the city, danger in the wilderness, danger at sea, danger from false brethren; in toil and hardship, through many a sleepless night, in hunger and thirst, often without food, in cold and exposure ...'[87]

'Not disobedient'!

What is particularly surprising is that it was Jesus whose followers he had been persecuting who spoke to him in his reveries on the road to Damascus. As a consequence of that vision a new spirit was let loose on the non-Jewish world, the spirit of the Jesus he had encountered.

For Paul became the most influential personality in the history of the church. From that decisive revelation on the road to Damascus his life was dominated by an ardent devotion to Christ, who was from then on the centre of his preaching, of his teaching and of this personal faith and life. We catch a glimpse of this when, later if life writing to the Philippians, he describes his earlier days and his standing

> '... circumcised on the eighth day, of the people of Israel, of the tribe of Benjamin, a Hebrew born of Hebrews; as to the law a Pharisee [the purifiers of corruption in the Judaism of the times], as to zeal a persecutor of the church, as to righteousness under the law blameless ...'

then he continues,

> 'But whatever gain I had, I counted as loss for the sake of

Christ. Indeed I count everything as loss because of the surpassing worth of knowing Christ Jesus my Lord. For his sake I have suffered the loss of all things, and count them as refuse, in order that I might gain Christ.'[88]

Paul had the best formal education of any of the New Testament writers in the Rabbinical schools of Jerusalem and as a Roman citizen of Tarsus. He was the one who providentially had the intellectual equipment, the ardour, the vocation and sheer endurance to take the good new of Jesus the Christ out of its initially Jewish environment and to make it available to the wider world.

Yet we have to admit that, like all ardent personalities, he evokes mixed feelings in us. It is sometimes said, not without justification, that the only way to avoid criticism in Oxford academic life is to talk about projects, and do nothing! Paul was not such a one and met opposition. We hear him tetchy, almost petulant sometimes, as he tries to answer his critics – whose who say all Christians have to fulfil the requirements of the Hebrew Torah; those who question the authenticity of his gospel and of his authority and authorisation; those who say the Christian community should not support its ministers or help the poor Christian community in Jerusalem, a cause dear to his heart.

Nevertheless, amazingly, refined as if by fire, we detect in him a mellowing and a widening of his vision and sympathies as we read his latter letters. Gradually he begins to exemplify in himself the manifestation in his life of that Spirit of Christ that he had encountered in the vision on the Damascus road.

What that vision involved we can best judge from the way it worked itself in his life and in the sheer intellectual muscle of his thinking and meditations. Supremely, it was an inclusive vision of the unification of all humanity through the action of God which had now become possible in human beings who made themselves open and obedient to God. This was now possible, Paul saw, because God had manifest and expressed himself in the human person of Jesus, and in and through him we see and meet God as unifying, self-offering, suffering Love.

This essentially Christian vision is firstly of the unification of the individual. In the 7th chapter of his letter to the Romans, we have an agonised account of a human being at odds with him-or herself and at odds with God (it may be autobiographical):

> 'For I do not do what I want, but I do the very thing I hate ... I can will what is right, but I cannot do it. For I do not do the good I want, but the evil I do not want is what I do ... For I delight in the law of God, in my inmost self, but I see in my members another law at war with the law of my mind and making me captive to the law of sin. Wretched man that I am! Who will deliver me from this body of death?'.[89]

And then Paul cries out, 'Thanks be to God through Jesus Christ our Lord'. We too can join in this cry of gratitude because in Jesus the Christ we have seen humanity released from such bondage by the very indwelling of God in a human being and that indwelling of God as Spirit waits to unify our inner selves too – to make us Christ-like, that is, human beings whose inner motivations resonate with God's own purposes.

But we as individuals have personalities, are persons, only because we live and flourish, or fade, in a nexus of interactions with other people. So the second feature of the Christian vision which is so prominent in Paul's writing is that of the unity of the church – that is, of Christ's Holy Catholic Church which is, as Oxford University's Bidding Prayer reminds us, 'the whole congregation of Christian people dispersed throughout the whole world'. Paul's world was smaller, but the divisions within his flock were just as real as those we have inherited from the centuries. Writing to those fractious and quarrelsome Corinthians, who had divided into a 'Paul party', an 'Apollos party', and a 'Cephas party', according to whoever had baptized them, Paul explodes: 'Is Christ divided?' and, at the end of a magnificent passage about the foolishness of God being wiser than the wisdom of humanity, affirms that, as a consequence

> 'no human being might boast in the presence of God. He is the source of your life in Christ Jesus, whom God made our wisdom, our righteousness and sanctification and redemption.'[90]

Even if history has bequeathed a variety of institutional expression of the faith, only a church which is visibly one in spirit and in action has any hope of making actual the third, and last, and greatest of the visions of unity that Paul had through Jesus Christ – that of all humanity. In his letter to the Galatians he wrote 'There is neither Jew nor Greek, there is neither slave nor free, there is neither male or female; for you are all one in Christ Jesus'.[91]

Paul struggled to break down the first of these barriers – that between Gentile and Jew – and he succeeded at least within the church. But it took eighteen centuries for Christendom to realize that slavery was totally inconsistent with the Gospel of Christ. And it has taken twenty centuries, for the church to recognize that women are not second-class human beings. Jesus had treated women as equals, to the surprise of his contemporaries, and Paul had made the principle explicit. He did, of course, accept the mores of his times (about women covering their heads, and not speaking in public occasions, and obeying their husbands) but again and again the principle I've quoted leads him to soften and liberate from these customs – so that Morna Hooker, professor of New Testament in Cambridge, used to have a sermon that she delighted to deliver entitled 'Paul – the Apostle of women's lib'! In Paul's vision human beings of all sorts and conditions should find their unity in the church and the role of the church is the reconciliation of human beings to each other under God.

These visions of Paul, which he spread and shared with the first-century followers of Jesus are entirely consistent with, and indeed can be shown to be consequences of what Jesus himself had taught about the character of God's Reign, God's Kingdom, ruling over the hearts and minds and souls of humanity. What Paul, along with other New Testament writers discerned was the crucial role in establishing God's Kingdom in the hearts and minds and souls of humanity of the unique manifestation of the nature of God to be found in that very person, Jesus the Christ, who had inducted them into it.

These are overwhelming visions that we encounter, then, in the life and writings of the Saul of Tarsus who became St Paul. Even if we ourselves do not have experiences like that of Saul on the

Damascus road (and do not be so sure that one never will!) there are, for all of us, those moments of self-knowledge and clarity when we see our lives in perspective, perhaps in the broader sweep of what God might be intending us to do with our lives *sub specie aeternitate*, in an eternal framework – those moments perhaps when we are half waking up and are still, and the mind roams freely contemplating who and what we are and are becoming – moments perhaps when we catch a glimpse of beauty in nature or in music – or are suddenly overwhelmed by mutual love with another person. We *do* have our encounters on the Damascus road. May we not be disobedient to our heavenly visions.

21

Suffering with God

'Man goeth to his long home and the mourners
go about the streets' (*Eccl. 12, v.5 AV*)

There can be few passages in ancient or modern literature that
convey to us more acutely and accurately the sense of despair that
can be generated by social desolation and disaster than the chapter that concludes the book of Ecclesiastes, the words of one
called simply the 'Preacher'. Even the most casual viewer of our
television screens has witnessed such scenes in famine-stricken
or war-ravaged parts of the globe, this latter experience not being
entirely foreign to us in these comfortable islands, at least to those
of us who remember the destruction of Second World War bomb-
ing in this country. With modern communications we are more
aware than any other previous generation of the scope and scale
of both natural disasters and of the perennial barbarity of human
inhumanity to other human beings.

Why so much suffering in the world? Why any suffering at all,
we cry to God? And then the thought strikes us, as it has done
multitudes down the ages, surely either God can but will not
prevent suffering; or God would be cannot do so. And then for
some the whole possibility of believing in God as Creator and as
essentially Love disintegrates into a despairing scepticism to
which even the 'Preacher' of Ecclesiastes did not succumb.

The dilemma is real and is rooted in profound misunderstand-
ings of the nature of the God worshipped in the Christian faith.
We have too easily attached ourselves to a concept of God that I
prefer to call 'the God of the philosophers' – the God who is
absolutely without change, or parts, without anything corresponding to feeling, remote, totally omnipotent, totally omniscient, dwelling in a realm unconnected with our space and time.
But this is not the God of the Judeo-Christian tradition and of the

Bible. For the Father of Abraham, Isaac and Jacob and the God and Father of our Lord Jesus Christ is 'a God who suffers eminently and yet is still God, and a God who suffers universally and yet is still present uniquely and decisively in the sufferings of Christ'[92]. Why and how can we say this?

Firstly, we obtain a significant insight from what we know of the natural world. In it chance operates in a lawlike framework that enables new forms, including living ones and so us, to emerge in the universe. This emergence of new forms of life is only through the costly processes of natural selection with the death of the old forms. Furthermore, the emergence of sensitive, free, intelligent persons is only possible through a development that inevitably involves increasing sensitivity to pain and the concomitant experience of suffering with a growing conscious-ness and self-consciousness. Moreover the very features of the world that we find so inimical as the source of individual suffer-ing (e.g., mutations in DNA causing cancer) are the very same processes that make the emergence of life, in general, and of human life, in particular, possible.

Nothing, of course, can diminish our sense of loss and tragedy as we experience or witness particular natural evils, especially in those we love and to whom we are near. In willing the end, the emergence of free persons, God cannot but will the means in a universe that is going to have any inbuilt creativity. But God does not do it without cost to Godself. For, since God is at work in, with and under these creative processes of the natural world and their costly, open-ended unfolding in time, we are led to a new insight, namely, that God's own self suffers in, with and under these events, especially those of sentient creatures, and pre-eminently ourselves.

So we begin to see dimly, and this is the second pointer, that there is a profound cost to God in the creating of the world, not least in his bringing into existence thereby created beings, human beings, that are persons who can freely come into communion with him and with each other – and can, equally freely, frustrate the divine purposes for them and the world (witness our global environmental crisis).

Because of the high destiny that God has for all of us, God took this risk in creation by making us free and so we begin to understand that in creating a world that leads to us, God took suffering upon Godself. But to act in a way costly to oneself on behalf of the ultimate good of another, even, indeed especially, when one is misunderstood, is precisely what, in ordinary human language, we regard as the ultimate expression of love towards the other. So we begin to perceive that God's acts of creation are an expression of costly 'love', an outgoing of God's inner being on behalf the 'others', that is, created persons. As the first Epistle of John says bluntly, 'God is love'.

Indeed, if God is at least personal (and personal language is the highest category of expression available to us to denote the transcendent divine Being), then the love of God must involve a suffering-with, a sym-pathy, with the suffering of those who are loved. It cannot be for God simply a matter of only his divine will giving existence to all-that-is, but must include something akin, in personal terms, to our feelings and reacting towards others who are suffering. This is, indeed, at a number of points the language of the Old Testament for the prophets again and again talk of God as grieving at the situations of his people that they have brought on themselves. God labours and suffers at the plight of Israel – most of all when it rejects his proffered love. So even here we begin to be brought to see that God is affected by our sufferings and reacts to them and so, unlike the 'God of the philosophers', undergoes changes in the divine experience, while remaining unchanged in his character of benevolent love for our ultimate good.

We are now ready to discern the third and final pointer to, indeed revelation of, the character of God as suffering, self-offered Love. All the foregoing – whether in the character and nature of the created, creating world, or our surmises about what divine Love could be like, or the experiences of the prophets of Israel – all these are only pointers, hints, surmises, considerations that dispose us to think that God might actually be alongside us in our sufferings. But in the life, passion and death of Jesus the Christ, the one human being who was totally open to God, and thus the fullest revelation of the character of God that was possible in the created world, in him we see an actualization in our history of what is eternally true of God's nature – the Cross in the experience of God's dealings with our world. It is a vast mistake, in view of our present awareness of the unity of the human person, and so of the person of Jesus, to divide Jesus up into a human 'nature' that can and did suffer and a divine 'nature' that, as it were, just looked on. No, the startling, salvific and healing revelation is that what we see in the life, death and passion of Jesus the Christ is that God's own self is not only like this but actually is his, namely self-offering Love that will go to any lengths to draw all people to communion with himself. The Cross expresses what is the most divine about God and what is eternally true of him – for God has himself chosen to be found by stricken humanity in the suffering and humiliation of the cross of Jesus the Christ. The seer of the Book of Revelation did not shrink from describing Christ as 'the Lamb slain from the foundation of the world'.[93] In the cross God has revealed in the only way possible what he is really like. Again we recall Paul Fiddes incisive expression of this insight: 'God suffers in the cross in *oneness* with the person of Christ; God suffers *eternally* in the cross; God is most *Godlike* in the suffering of the cross'.[94]

Amongst the dismal record of man's inhumanity to man, nothing can have surpassed in the annals of human suffering the experience of the Jewish people in the Holocaust of the Nazi concentration camps. A survivor of Auschwitz, Elie Weisel, relates[95] how one day the SS guards hanged two Jewish men and a young boy in front of the whole camp. The men died quickly, but the child did not. Weisel recalls, ' "Where is God? Where is He?" someone behind me asked'. For more than half an hour the death agony was prolonged. Weisel continues 'Behind me, I heard the same man asking: "Where is God now?" And I heard a voice within me answer him: "Where is He? here He is – He is hanging here on this gallows".'

It is this profound insight that can transform our attitude to and sympathy with suffering. When we suffer, it is open to us voluntarily to take our place within the being of God because God has suffered in the cross, for we can now recognize our own suffering as belonging to God as well.

From our reflection on the nature of the world we saw that God has made the world as it is because he chooses to suffer with it. We need to remind ourselves too of the further, revealed truth that the humanity of Jesus the Christ has been transformed through self-offering love and taken up into the very life of God. That is what the Ascension is about in all its symbolic history. So there is now within the very being of God a memory of what it is to suffer as a human being and this awareness in the life of God is now one with that self-offering, suffering love that sustains all-that-is. When we suffer, when those we love suffer, when our sym-pathy extends to others outside our immediate circle who suffer, we can now know that God is suffering with us and them. 'God is the great companion – the fellow-sufferer who understands', said A. N. Whitehead in 1929[96], thereby reviving an old insight that had been suppressed in Christian thinking. But we can know also, not only that God suffers with us, but that in the person of the divinised humanity of Jesus there has occurred victory over suffering. For the suffering of God is a creative suffering. God has manifested his creative intentions for humanity in the self-offered life, the humiliating passion and shameful death of the one human being who was and is totally one with the being of God. That manifest suffering revealed itself as creative in the Resurrection of the human Jesus and as victorious by his being taken up into the life of God in the Ascension.

Thus it is that, in the light of Christ, when we suffer, when those we love suffer, when the world around us suffers, we can know that God suffers with us and for us. And we can know that, if we throw ourselves entirely on to God, the fellow-sufferer who understands, he will give us victory over the suffering by trans-forming us. Then we can share in his life both now and beyond the grave.

> 'The Spirit of God affirms to our spirit that we are God's children; and if children, then heirs, heirs of God and fellow-heirs with Christ; but we must share his sufferings if we are also to share his glory. For I reckon that the sufferings we now endure bear no comparison with the glory, as yet unre-vealed, which is in store for us ... For I am convinced that there is nothing in death or life, in the realm of spirits or

superhuman powers, in the world as it is or the world as it shall be, in the forces of the universe, in heights or depths – nothing in all creation that can separate us from the love of God in Christ Jesus our Lord.'[97]

22

Sharing in Creation

'For he [God] is the guide even of wisdom and the
corrector of the wise. For both we and our words are in
his hands, as are all understanding and skill in crafts ...
For she [Wisdom] is a breath of the power of God, and
a pure emanation of the glory of the Almighty.'

(Wisdom 8, vv. 15,15,25; NRSV)

In a glorious spring some years ago, I was fortunate enough to be
touring in Italy the hill towns of Umbria and Tuscany. I was overwhelmed by the sheer beauty of the towns and villages that grew
out of those rocky mountains tops and of the creativity of the
Italian people in that period we call the Renaissance. For, in spite
of the depredations of the centuries, there were to be found the
most wonderful and luminous frescoes – not only those of Giotto
in a grand church such as that of the Basilica of St Francis of
Assisi, but also unsuspectingly in small places – as when we
entered what seemed to be a dark and dismal church in the little
village of Spello, and switching on the lights in a small side
chapel, were overwhelmed by a blaze of colour and of the living
activity on the walls, painted by Pinturicchio in 1501. And so
much of this beauty is in the churches and devoted to enhancing
them. What, one could not help asking, was the relation of this
creative activity in art and architecture to the faith so evidently
symbolised in the churches and its fitments?

There can be no doubt that these creative artists saw no contra-
diction between the practice of their art and their faith, for we saw
this unity spelled out in stone in two magnificent thirteenth-
century pulpits, one in Siena and the other in Pisa, the work of the
Pisano family. Both of these splendid walled platforms, with their
lecterns from which the word of God was to be proclaimed, were
supported on elaborate arrangements of pillars depicting the

149

substructure, one might say, that underlies the proclamation of the Gospel. In addition to the obvious representations of prophets and Evangelists, these supports include representations of the arts of the Trivium and Quadrivium, the seven Liberal Arts – grammar, rhetoric and logic and arithmetic, geometry, astronomy and music – both the prolegomena to the study of theology and its cultural support.

Here we were seeing the visible representation of the spirit of that re-won Christian humanism of the Italian Renaissance. This came to be expressed verbally and more explicitly by some later fifteenth-century Florentine writers (Manetti and Ficino) whose concept of the creation of human beings in the image of God and whose vision of humanity's heavenly destiny represented 'an important new conception of man as actor, creator, shaper of nature and history, all of which qualities he possesses for the very reason that he is made 'in the image and likeness' of the Trinity'.[98]

This is the germ of the idea of human beings sharing in the creative work of God – being, as it were, co-creators with God, but not with a capital 'C' for human creativity is a created and derived creativity, endowed by God the Creator, spelt with capital 'C'. The thinkers and creative artists of the Renaissance were in fact recovering something already implicit in the biblical tradition and specifically expressed in its Wisdom literature, the significance of which is only now again being recovered in recent biblical scholarship. Thus in the passage from the seventh chapter of the *Wisdom of Solomon*, which includes the quotation given at the start, we find the basis of a profound re-evaluation of the creativity of humanity. In that remarkable and famous passage, and indeed throughout that book. 'Wisdom' is the female personification of the outgoing activity of God in all creation, an activity that is mirrored in the creative activity of that part of creation capable of responding to God and able itself also to be creative – namely human beings. Later this activity came to be denoted as that of the Holy Spirit of God particularly present in Jesus the Christ.

Today the scientific perspective on the world and life as evolving and developing has resuscitated for our time an earlier tradition of divine creation as continuous. And the interplay of chance and law in this creative and creating process leads us now to stress the open-ended character of the emergence of new forms. I have tried[99] to articulate this through the model of God as the composer of the fugue of creation, as the leader in a dance of creation, and as exploring all the possibilities and as actualizing potentialities in a spirit of delight and play. We recognise now that creation is still going on – the fugue is still unfolding in time – the choreography is still being elaborated.

But – and here is the question implicit in this – what of human beings in this process? We find ourselves with creative energies both within ourselves and in relation to nature through our technology – do we join in the creative work of God harmoniously integrating our own material and other creations into what God is already doing? Or are we going to be source of discord in the harmony of creation, the origin of confusion within its developing dance?

Humanity is now faced with the possibility of acting as a participant in creation, of being, as it were, the leader of the orchestra of creation in the performance that is God's continuing composition. Human beings with their new powers of technology and with new scientific knowledge of the world's ecosystems could, if they chose, become that part of God's creation consciously and intelligently co-operating with God's intentions in the continuing process of creative change – taking due account both of the needs of humanity and of the rest of the natural order. But what can we know of those intentions?

Christians are those who believe, and think they have grounds for so believing, that God the Creator has expressed God's meaning and intentions, not only in the intricate and ramified levels of created nature, but supremely, explicitly and openly in the life, death and resurrection of a unique being in the created world – Jesus of Nazareth. He was so completely open to God that God filled his human nature and revealed its potentialities. For it has always been understood among Christians that Jesus was fully and completely human and from this it follows that one of the principal meanings of his life, death and resurrection (and teaching) for us is that the transcendent Creator can be immanent in a human being at the fully personal level. God's work of re-creation of humanity that occurred in Jesus the Christ can be continued in us, and indeed in what we appropriately call our 'recreation' – that is, those activities in which are creative potentialities have free scope. When we as persons are most creative – whether in the arts, science, technology, literature, in intellectual reflection, in our work, or in personal and social relations, our distinctively human activities – then we are fulfilling those human potentialities that were unveiled in Jesus uniquely as the continuous work of God in humanity. Human beings have a creativity derived from God, the inspiration of the God as Spirit, and all genuine human activities which attain excellence and are in accord with God's intentions to build God's reign of love, God's 'kingdom', may then be seen as humanity exerting its role as a co-creator with God. As William Blake would have said, in exercising our God-given creative capabilities we are 'building Jerusalem'. We recall that marvellous series of illustrations of his for the Book of Job. It begins with Job and his family depicted as worshipping God – so-called 'worship' Blake would have us understand – all of them sitting under the Tree of Life from which hang musical instruments, as 'untouched as on a Calvinist Sabbath', as Kathleen Raine describes them. After Job's redemption through suffering and restoral to full life, the family all now stand under the Tree playing the instruments and enthusiastically joining in making the music of both heaven and earth. As Kathleen Raine writes in her percipient study

> 'The series begins and ends with a symbolic expression of Blake's belief that the Christianity is "the liberty both of body and of mind to exercise the Divine Arts of Imagination ... Let every Christian, as much as in him lies, engage himself openly and publicly before all the World in some mental pursuit for the Building up of Jerusalem" ... In the last plate each has taken his instrument, and all are playing and singing with that joyful and tireless industry of spirit which for Blake was the essence of Christianity.' [100]

For those who believe in God as Creator are bound to recognize, if they reflect on the consequences of their belief, that it must have been God's intentions that human society should have attained its present economic, social and technological complexity, for Godself endowed us with the capabilities that made it inevitable. But we as Christians also believe that this Creator God was expressed fully in a human person and thereby showed the primacy of the personal in the divine creative purpose. Our capabilities – the individually creative ones I've already mentioned and the socially, economically and technologically complex ones – are to be exercised for the enhancement and enrichment of all creation, in general, and supremely of the personal in creation.

The Christians can therefore see his or her work, not simply as a kind of sacrificial offering to God as past piety has often represented it, but in this wider perspective now afforded us it can be seen as a genuine 'work of God', an *opus Dei* in its own right. For in building up human society, human togetherness, one is joining in the creative activity of God that made all life, including human life, possible. Even the humblest job in the complex society created by technology in satisfaction of real and legitimate needs would take on a new point if seen as part of that creative process that brought humanity and society into existence. Provision of such a wider context could, in principle at least, give a new significance to daily work and so counteract the pointlessness and vacuousness that so many feel about it. Isn't this what we need to give a renewed sense of vocation in our daily work?

As Teilhard de Chardin put it:

> 'There was reason to fear that ... the seeking after, and waiting for, the kingdom of heaven might deflect human activity from its natural tasks ... Now we see why this cannot and must not be so ... God does not deflect our gaze prematurely from the work he himself has given us, since he presents himself to us as attainable through that very work ... God, in all that is most living and incarnate in him, is not far away from us, altogether apart from the world we see and touch, hear, smell and taste about us. Rather he awaits us in every instant in our action, in the work of the moment. There is a sense in which he is at the tip of my pen, my spade, my brush, my needle – of my heart and of my thoughts.' [101]

Why should there not, along with traditional avowals we associate with the life of the Church, be those who are vowed to the task of exemplifying by their lives, the general sanctification of human endeavour? – those whose common Christian ideal would be to give a full and conscious exemplification of the divine possibilities or demands which any worldly occupation implies – those who would devote themselves in the fields of thought, art, industry, agriculture, commerce and politics, etc., to carry out in the Spirit of God these demands, the basic tasks that form the very bonework of human society?

Such an apprehension of the possibility of a life of humanity engraced by God does now, in the light of what I've said about God's creative action in the world, allow us to make a more positive assessment of human civilization, in general, and of technology, in particular. For it is not without significance that the Bible begins with creation out of physical chaos and is consummated in the new Jerusalem – a city, symbol of human culture.

So let us join with William Blake in asking God to enable us to cooperate with him in 'building up Jerusalem'. To do this we certainly need that holy spirit of wisdom and we cannot but pray:

'O God of the father, and Lord who keepest thy mercy; who madest all things by thy word and by thy wisdom ... formest mankind ... Give me wisdom, her that sitteth by thee on thy throne; and reject me not from among thy servants' (Wisdom 9, vv. 1,2,4).

23

Hope in Life

There is a natural human curiosity and enchantment about the future – for it is undoubtedly true that is where we all plan to spend the rest of our lives! Yet do not most of us feel, now, that even the future isn't what it used to be? The hopeful 1960s – the decade of Kennedy, of Vatican II – of the first space-flights to the moon gave way to the tried cynicism of the 1970s as the hopes placed in these features of our life became increasingly manifest as misplaced; and so to the materialism of the 1980s and the confusions of this decade. As Jurgen Moltmann said in the 1970s, and it still applies today:

> 'Everywhere people feel deceived, abused, dispirited, exploited, and estranged so that they no longer trust the inbuilt goals and hopes of our progressive societies, universities, churches and sciences. They refuse to live goal-orientated and future-conscious, since they refuse to freeze that future in its present image.'[102]

Hope has become one of the lost virtues of our age and its loss infects every aspect of our cultural and social life. 'Where there is no vision, the people perish'[103] applies as ever. In the Western industrialised world, the sensitive experience *angst* and despair, and the insensitive indulge in a frantic search for substitute ends – in domestic mechanisation and other manifestations of private affluence, in elaborate holidays, in lethal speeds, in world-escaping religions of personal salvation, in astrology and space fiction and even in the occult. Ironically, if we, the Western and industrialised, are the oppressors, it is clear that the struggle for freedom from our oppression at least gives the oppressed of the Third World meaning to life and hope for the future. Those in control of the world's resources of power become more and more apprehensive of the future. We suspect that 'we've never had it so good' and we'll never have it again. There seems to be a widespread loss of faith in the ability of the future to bring something which is actually more fulfilling into human life. Many thinking people fear that what they have experienced as the 'Death of God' is being followed by the 'Death of Humanity' as human spontaneity becomes paralysed and as humanity becomes interred in a tomb of technical-economic structures of its own making. Increasingly many feel that the Orwellian '1984' is already with us.

But not only have people lost hope in the future – they have lost hope in themselves. Many have come to take a reduced view, indeed a reductionist one, of their humanity – they see themselves as nothing but bipedal terrestrial mammals, tool-making naked apes, gene machines programmed for the survival of their selfish genes, homeostatic mechanisms equipped with language-programmed computers.

Some sociobiologists and philosophers of biology, to avoid such minimising accounts of humanity, have emphasised, with the biologist Richard Dawkins, that human beings produce entities (ideas, habits, melodies, visual symbols – 'memes') which also have survival value within the community of human brains – and survive in a distinctive way in what the philosopher of science, Karl Popper, has called 'World 3' (the world of libraries, records, the 'media'). This certainly begins to give some recognition that *homo sapiens* is the one biological organism who is also a self-conscious person, but such considerations do now come within light-years of meeting the real question. For ideas, the products of the creative mind, only survive in the structures of civilisation if they have some basic appeal to us – and they only have that if they really satisfy our needs and fulfil our aspirations. But to ask them to do this is to ask, to use the haunting title of a famous story by Tolstoy, 'What do men live by?'

What, when the chips are down, do men and women really need to live their lives *with* hope – without that despairing, frantic vacuous aimlessness and shapelessness that characterises so many lives today – both young and old alike, even when their basic biological needs of food, rest, shelter and sex are satisfied. Apart from these basic biological needs – and our affluent and permissive Western societies evidence only too clear that *angst* and despair prevailing even when these *are* satisfied – there are certain perennial human needs which stand out as the boundary markers of the territory and span of human life. I discern four such:

We need to come to terms with our own death. Human beings, alone of all biological creatures, have been concerned with death and been aware of the affront to their personal self-consciousness that dissolution of their bodily frames threatens. But it is not generalisation of the kind 'man is mortal' that really bite. As Ivan Ilyich recalls in another story of Tolstoy (*The death of Ivan Ilyich*): 'Caius is a man, men are mortal, therefore Caius is mortal', but with a shock he [Ivan] realises '... That Caius – man in the abstract – was mortal, was perfectly correct, but I am not Caius, not an abstract man, but a creature, quite, quite separate from all others ... It cannot be that I ought to die. That would be too terrible'.[104] Every one of us will in the end be identified with materiality and it appears as though the universe will go on its way as though we had never been born. Or will it? That is the question to which we need an answer.

We need to come to terms with our finitude. The awareness of death is but the most intense of a number of other experiences of finitude: experiences of human physical limitations: in encounter with material objects and, more recently, in encounter with the extent of space and time in the observed universe; in experiences of organic limitation (illness, exhaustion, failure, etc.); in experiences of personal limitation (in clashes with the wills of other persons, in decisions, etc.); and in experiences of normative constraints, in trying to make distinctions such as true/false, right/wrong and ugly/beautiful. Realism accepts these limitations, but frequently these experiences of our finitude themselves push us to a sense of our ultimate limit which acts as a medium through which is challenged the very way in which we regard our own personal identity. This awareness of our finitude is an incongruity between us and our niche in the world and it is not accounted for, or satisfied within, the biological as such.

We need to learn how to bear suffering. Our self-awareness has as a concomitant the rendering almost intolerable of our experience of suffering, whether in ourselves or in other people, and even in the non-human world. Although various considerations may mollify us intellectually, we nevertheless wonder whether the pain and suffering we see in biological life, in general, and in human beings, in particular, can be justified in any way that satisfies our moral sense. Finally:

We need to realise our potentialities and to steer our path through life – to put it bluntly, we want to be successful, and not failures. Yet we are only too well aware of our failure to become what we might be and what we ought to be. We are to ourselves unfulfilled paradoxes. Individually we ask more urgently than ever before. 'What should I be striving to become?' that is, 'What am I for?' We are indeed unique among living organisms in being able to choose our direction and to ask ourselves such questions. It is at this very point that we are enigmas to ourselves – never better expressed than by St Paul when, in that famous outburst in the 7th chapter of his letter to the Romans.

We may well ask – what did, indeed what does, God think God is up to in evolving and sustaining human beings, the 'glory, jest and riddle of the world'[105] with their enormous potentialities for good and evil and saddled with those in-built needs which seem incapable of being satisfied?

St Paul claims 'God was reconciling the world to himself' and goes on to urge us to 'be reconciled to God'.[106] But to be reconciled also to death, finitude, suffering and failure? I suggest that to be reconciled 'to God' is to be reconciled to these too. The only reason *that* can be claimed is because we can now know that God is the God who is the 'Father of our Lord Jesus Christ' – that in Jesus the Christ we encounter a human being, so open to the God who is the ultimate Reality in and behind all-that-is, that God was able personally to unveil Godself as the love who suffers in, with, through and for creation. Thereby God can bring to realisation in human creation all its potentialities and possibilities – potentialities and possibilities unimagined hitherto by human beings but always buried deep in the purposes of God. For Jesus the road that

led to resurrection and ascension – rising from the life of humanity to dwell in the very presence of God – was a path that led
through the experience and acceptance of death, finitude, suffering and failure. In those hard realities God – spite of all appear-
ances and indeed, in spite of his own psychological awareness
('My God, my God, why have you forsaken me'[107]) – God was
able to bring him, this one person, Jesus, into a communion with
Himself which transcends all previously constricted possibilities
of humankind.

In other words, God who is the circumambient Reality who
pervades and sustains all existence, and all modes of human existence, was present, creating and structuring the very pattern of
events which brought Jesus into his Presence. In our experience
of death, finitude, suffering and failure, too, God is the Reality
who is breaking through to us – but for the life, death, resurrection
and ascension of Jesus it would have been only this 'dark side of
God', as it has been called, that we would have encountered in
such experiences.

But now, thanks be to God, through the revelation that is in
Jesus (whom we therefore name the 'Christ', the anointed One of
God) we know that human death is but the opening of a door to a
wider life with God; that in suffering we are never alone for God
himself is in it with us; that our finitude can find its place in the
plenitude of the communion of saints in the presence of God; that
our criteria of success and failure are completely irrelevant to
God who reaches out to respond to all those who seek him,
regardless of human standards.

Thus we learn through Jesus the Christ that God is not only the
ultimate Reality to whom all things revert 'in the end', but that he
is the present Reality in, with, through and under the bitterest of
our experiences.

In the experience of Christ, God was truly present and this is
the token, pledge and means whereby God is present with us in
those experiences – thus can we through Jesus the Christ be
reconciled to the Reality that is the God who is bringing creation
to fulfilment through self-offering Love.

And so we can have hope in life, after all – in whatever life can
bring. Because we now know, that – whatever we may feel, or

surmise, or predict, or rebel against and flee from – in the depths
of our direct experience God is present to suffer with us, to raise
us to new life and to take us into God's presence – in God's good
time. For God may not hurry – but never fails.

In the words of the sermon that John Donne preached in St
Paul's on Christmas Day in the Evening, 1624:

'God made Sun and Moon to distinguish seasons, and day,
and night, and we cannot have the fruits of the earth but in
their seasons: But God hath made no decree to distinguish
the seasons of his mercies; In paradise, the fruits were ripe,
the first minute, and in heaven it is alwaies Autumn, his
mercies are ever in their maturity. We ask *panem quotidi-
anum*, our daily bread, and God never sayes you should have
come yesterday, he never sayes you must againe tomorrow,
but *today if you will heare his voice*, today he will heare you.
If some King of the earth have so large an extent of
Dominion, in North, and South, as that he hath Winter and
Summer together in his Dominions, so large an extent East
and West, as that he hath day and night together in his
Dominions, much more hath God mercy and judgement
together: He brought light out of darknesse, not out of a
lesser light; he can bring thy Summer out of Winter, though
thou have no Spring; though in the wayes of fortune, or
understanding, or conscience, thou have been benighted till
now, wintred and frozen, clouded and eclypsed, damped
and benummed, smothered and stupified till now, and god
comes to thee, not as in the dawning of the day, not as in
the bud of the spring, but as the Sun at noon to illustrate all
shadowes, as the sheaves in harvest, to fill all penuries, all
occasions invite his mercies, and all times are his
seasons.'[108]

PART III

EXPLORATIONS

24

The Old and the New
(an Oxford University Sermon)

Those who are involved in, or interested in, national politics, or even academic politics, need no reminding that there is in all of us both a radical and a conservative element. As the contemplative night sentry guarding the Houses of Parliament tells us in 'Iolanthe':

> 'Every boy and every gal that's born into the world alive
> Is either a little Liberal or else a little Conservative.'

Whether or not he was right in thinking that adoption of radical or conservative views was simply a matter of Nature, we all recognise that we oscillate between love of the new and love of the old; we are all radical about some things and conservative about others. A radical in national politics may be an arch-conservative in academic matters, as we all know, and vice versa.

This rhythm of mood and attitude is in fact necessitated as we find ourselves adapting to new situations in the light of our former ideas and experiences. More generally, our Western societies today reveal an almost unprecedented and frenetic search for new supposed 'realities', a search that generates a babble of conflicting voices. In this supermarket of ideas, many delicately select according to their own pre-conceived notions or, as from a smorgasbord, make their own mix according to taste – from among the panaceas of Divine Light, Transcendental Meditation, 'Unification' religion, Theosophy, serial music, jogging or aerobics. Within this cacophony two voices continue to ring out because they represent two poles of human experience and because they gain a universal audience – the older voice of religion and the newer one of science.

Taking this latter first, for the last three hundred years the mounting success of the scientific method of examining nature in prediction and control has made it seem for many the vary paradigm of truth and of the only kind truth really accessible to humanity. It has seemed to them that the analytical method of scientific research, whereby wholes are broken down into investigatable parts, would reveal the very foundation stones of our existence and make all intelligible. And yet the actual entities which constitute the stuff of modern science are extraordinarily variegated and enigmatic in their status. For these entities of the 'real' world that science now reveals include not only the circulation of the blood, bacteria, water as H_2O, relatively familiar molecules and even visualisable atoms, but also such entities as quasars, black holes, quarks, electron holes, anti-matter, gravitational waves, spin, 'charm' and many other mysterious entities – and even a vacuum containing no matter, or radiation, we are now told, can be an immense reservoir of energy. Although a long training and intensive research can familiarise practitioners with these terms, so they come to be for them almost household names, a more objective analysis of the use of scientific language and its intellectual techniques has increasingly emphasised in recent years the metaphorical nature of all scientific language and its use of models as generators of such language. Any naïvely realistic view of the language of science has long since been shattered by the revolution in physics that took place in the first decades of this century. The language of science is metaphorical and is always revisable *but* it is still the aim of science to depict reality as best it can and to produce concepts and ideas which are at least candidates for reality. The whole enterprise would grind to a halt unless most workers in most laboratories did not think they really were making an exploration into the nature of reality, however tentative.

But what about the religious quest of humanity?

Ever since the emerging species of *homo sapiens* buried its dead with ritual, humanity has displayed an awareness of the tragedy of the ephemeral, the reality and yet the inner unacceptability of the cycle of life and death, and has sought a transcendent meaning in another Reality for that brief flickering into self-consciousness which all its members experience. Thus the religious quest of mankind, its long search for meaning and significance, is still one of the most characteristic features of all societies – and I do not exclude our own, for there is a God-shaped room in the interior castle of every Western soul, and once empty and ungarnished, a plethora of new twentieth-century devils rush in to fill it. So here then is an exploration, a life-long one, an exploration 'into God' to be undertaken by every human being. Indeed, more specifically, this is what has been described as the essence of the *Christian* life – 'Christian life is an adventure, a voyage of discovery, a journey, sustained by faith and hope, towards the final and complete communion with Love at the heart of all things'.[11] Of course it is also the Christian affirmation that, in some sense, Jesus the Christ himself is in the words attributed to him in the fourth Gospel, 'the Way, the Truth and the Life.'

Here there are two claimed ways of exploring truth, truth about the natural world and truth about God – a new and an old way.

But, how do we relate the new knowledge to old wisdom not only in these two spheres but in the whole range of our intellectual life? This problem of relating different kinds of explanation and the different kinds of knowledge they attain is endemic to the very fabric of university life today. Furthermore our confusions about the relations between different kinds of knowledge become acutely and painfully exposed when there is controversy about ethical problems raised by advances, in particular, in the biological and medical sciences and debates about the wisdom of applying the new techniques they devise. The intensive debate, for example, about *in vitro* fertilisation and the legitimacy or otherwise of doing research on fertilised human ova, even in the first fourteen days of their existence, illustrates our public and private confusions. Is a complex of a countable number of cells to be regarded differently if the DNA contained in those proliferating cells happen to come from human beings rather than from some other species? If so, why? Any analysis of the biochemical level shows an extraordinary similarity of growing mammalian embryos at this stage. Or do we wait until these cells start to manifest the beginnings of a nervous system which, in its developed form, we know to be the transmitters of the sense of pain or pleasure and other signals? Or do we take note of the fact that, although these cells are not going to be allowed to develop into a human foetus and are in fact stored in such a way that this is impossible, these cells derive their component DNA and genetic information from Mr and Mrs X who in helping these cells to be created were hoping to have an offspring otherwise denied to them? At what level does this conglomeration of cells demand to be treated as a person with full human rights? Or do we accord it less than legal personal status and do not convict Nature of murder as it habitually discards a high proportion of such growing fertilised human ova? Do we, in affirming that a human being is more than just a particular aggregate of cells, go on to assert that there is an entity called the 'soul' which is associated with such a fully developed human being and that there must be a definite point in time at which that soul, the carrier of human distinctiveness, is attached to or associated with that growing conglomeration of cells? If so, when – at fertilisation, at fourteen days, the beginning of the nervous system, the beginning of the first movement of the foetus, actual physical birth into the world and separation from the mother?

I do not need to elaborate any further, for the intensity and emotional loading of the public debates shows only too well how much we lack a map of knowledge which would help us to relate ancient human wisdom and insights about the nature and destiny of human beings to their physiological, biochemical and genetic constitution.

Even with science itself a naïve reductionism that simply tries to account for the behaviour and properties of complex wholes entirely in terms of the knowledge of the separated parts breaks down. Witness the resistance by biologists who are ecologists or ethologists to simplistic interpretations that biology is nothing but physics and chemistry; witness also the resistance of sociologists to the corresponding take-over bid by geneticists who believe they can explain the complexity of human behaviour by cost-benefit analysis of the results of genetic exchange. Witness too, further up the scale the resistance of psychology to being taken over by neuro-physiology.

And so one could go on. It seems fairly clear now that the

hierarchy of complexity in the natural world, including human beings, is of such a kind that, with increasing complexity both of the individual organism and of its social and environmental ramifications, simplistic attempts to explain the whole in terms of the parts break down. New concepts and new methods of analysis become obligatory. Various slices are possible through the cake of reality but the slices that produce the smallest crumbs do not have the flavour of the whole.

If then we now accept that different levels in the complexities of the natural world, including the human and social, require different concepts and different modes of investigation and the concepts that are found to be relevant to any level of enquiry refer, however haltingly and metaphorically, to realities operative at those different levels, then might not there now be possible a new placing for theology in the whole intellectual exercise of humanity? For theology, insofar as it is reflection on that reality which is ultimate to both nature and man, must be operating at a level of integration which incorporates all the lesser levels of complexity of the social, the human, the psychological, the physiological, the biological and the physical. Theology is the intellectual articulation of the religious experience of mankind and this has supremely been concerned with contemplating, in their relation to God, both the character of human existence and the realities of nature. Theology, therefore, has to incorporate into its purview both the wisdom of the humanities, in their reflection on the richness and creativity of human experience, and the perspectives of the various sciences, with their respective accounts of the levels of complexity of the natural world, including *homo sapiens*.

But because theology deals with the ultimate realities, or more strictly, the ultimate Reality, it can properly claim to develop a language and concepts of its own in dealing with the content of the religious experience of humanity, that experience which tries to see the whole as a unity in relation to human destiny. So altogether theology certainly cannot, and should not, claim to be an autocratic queen of the sciences or of the humanities, perhaps it might at least aspire to becoming a constitutional moderator of them all. Certainly, it has, more than any other study, a vested interest in clarification of the relationship between different kinds of knowledge, whether these concern the natural world or the experience of humanity. It was an awareness of this which led the late Ian Ramsey from this very pulpit[109] in a University sermon to propound the need for a centre for the study of theology in relation to the whole range of the intellectual life of our times. This wider proposal took the particular form of the Centre[110] named after him, with an initial concern, during its first decade of operation, for the ethical problems raised by scientific and medical research and practice and now concentrating on interdisciplinary study of the relation of religious beliefs to the sciences, including medicine.

It is no use now seeking an occupant for the throne vacated by medieval theology but the intellectual exchange of a modern university desperately needs, it seems to me, the allocation of time, and that means of money, to enable investigators in all realms of knowledge to devote some of their energies to relating their knowledge to other disciplines and to creating a contemporary map of knowledge. This has always been the dream of a few ever since the collapse of the medieval synthesis but the quest has for many seemed hopeless with the increasing mechanistic world view that it was thought the natural sciences validated. But in recent decades there have deep subterranean shifts in many of the sciences and I think these are beginning to alter the visible landscape in which the activities of humanists and theologians are to be located. For that landscape now depicts a world in which what we have previously called insentient matter is now seen to have – through its own inherent self-organising properties and strictly within the laws of the thermodynamics of open systems – the capacity to generate entities of increasingly complexity, sensitivity, awareness and self-awareness, culminating in the humanity that is able to discern the very process by which it has emerged in the world. This humanity has, too, a creativity which includes not only an ability to manipulate the natural world but also the creativity of its own thought forms that produce the world of art and drama and literature and music, and indeed, science itself. Humanity has evolved along with and in complex ecosystems of both the

biological and inorganic worlds which are interlocked in mutually supportive relations, of the subtleties of which we are only
now beginning to get an inkling.

More and more the sciences are having to take a more holistic
and synthetic view of living organisms in their individuality and
in their complex inter-relationships as communities of organisms,
both homogeneous and heterogeneous. Furthermore, study of
matter, the very bits of the world stuff of which living organisms
are composed, is impelling the particle physicist and cosmologist
into realms of thought and speculation where processes and relationships begin to dominate their conceptual schemes and the
mechanical world of Newtonian physics and Daltonian, or should
I say Democritan, atoms recedes into insignificance. Any belief in
God as Creator cannot avoid taking into account this new
perspective on the created order. Instead of seeing God as a
remote *deux ex machina* who, as it were, wound up the clock of
the universe and left it to run, we now see that the process of
creation is still going on unfolding its possibilities in an open-
ended, indeed sometimes to us unpredictable, even playful, ways.
God is involved in, with and under this process, with all the
limitations that that implies – and Godself is now to be seen as
suffering in, with and under that process of creation to participation in which God calls humanity. Is not this ultimately what
the life, death and resurrection of Jesus the Christ mean? In such
a perspective the knowledge afforded by the sciences and that of
human experiences transmitted and studied by the humanities are
in tune with a new understanding of God as the orchestrator and
indeed theme-giver of the whole harmonious enterprise.

I have taken a large canvas and painted with a broad brush in
these last reflections. But I hope at least they give a hint of the
kind of reward that might be vouchsafed to those who are
prepared to risk the cold winds to which they may be exposed as
they bring their particular discipline out of the warmth of its own
coterie into the wider discourse of what might then properly be
called a *uni*-versity. Theology, supremely, should itself be willing
to take such a risk, for it is in the end the risk that the founder of
that Christian faith (which theology expounds) himself took in the
open commitment of his own life to manifesting God's presence

on earth – and which he testified was the characteristic of all those who were willing to participate in that kingdom, that reign of God, he was inaugurating. The university, in general, and theology, in particular, needs – with the help of God *semper Creator* – to be as the learner in the kingdom of Heaven who 'is like a householder who can produce from his store both the new and the old'.[111]

25

The Challenge of Science to the Thinking Church

'What most characterises the decline of faith in Britain is the perceived loss of credibility of religious belief, because it seems to have no foothold in a philosophical world view where the whole of reality can be encompassed by science' wrote the religious affairs correspondent of *The Times* in 1988.[112] Indeed surveys show that most young people in England and Scotland give up 'religion' because of 'science'. From a wider viewpoint, the historian Herbert Butterfield in his introduction to some Cambridge lectures even in 1948 could declare that the scientific revolution 'outshines everything since the rise of Christianity and reduces the Renaissance and the Reformation to the rank of mere episodes, mere internal displacements, within the system of medieval Christendom'.[113] It is the impact of this revolution on religious belief and, in particular, on Christianity, which bore the brunt of it, that is my concern here.

It is a fact in our society, that the media still propagate, almost unconsciously, a 'warfare' image of the relation between science and faith, as evidenced every time the British Association meets, when there unfailingly appear gleeful, and historically inaccurate, accounts of the encounter at its 1860 meeting between T. H. Huxley and the then Bishop of Oxford, Samuel Wilberforce. To this day it is still not regarded as professionally respectable for a biologist to admit to being a Christian. Did we not witness in Britain, in April, 1992, a contemporary biologist, Richard Dawkins, in the role of a Huxley-*redivivus*, attempting scornfully to denounce religion as represented by the then Archbishop of York, Dr John Habgood, actually himself formerly a physiologist? (The occasion was the Edinburgh International Festival of Science). It was interesting to observe the anti-religious and biassed reporting the occasion received from the science correspondents of even the broadsheets. This provoked articles and counter-articles, letters and comments in all the media – all good rollicking stuff, showing that 'science *versus* religion' was still regarded as a news-worthy sport. The proper concern should be, of course, with the actual state of their relationship. For it is as true today as it was some 60 years ago when A. N. Whitehead, the mathematician-philosopher, then said 'the future course of history would depend on the decision of his generation as to the proper relations between science and religion – so powerful were the religious symbols through which men and women conferred meaning on their lives, and so powerful the scientific models through which they could manipulate their environment.'[114]

In spite of several decades of sophisticated and informed analyses of the true contemporary state of the complex and subtle relationships between science and religion the idea that it is a state of 'conflict' still endures in the popular mind. Hence the views of young people in England and Scotland already reported are scarcely surprising. As we read the reports of that debate, we could not avoid realising that different perspectives were operating in the arguments concerning the actual status of scientific and religious affirmations and what counts as evidence for them. Indeed one of the most telling points in Dr Habgood's trenchant and at times withering response to Dawkins, when he had at last a chance to operate on a level playing field in the columns of the *Independent*, was that 'teasing out the relationship between these different kinds of knowledge, and exposing the fatal consequences of a lopsided concentration on only one kind, is a task for philosophy.'[115] A vital aspect of the relation of science to religion is indeed to sort out what kind of knowing they each represent – and this is as much a challenge to science as it is to religion.

In a post-modern age, science itself has come under attack as being sociologically and ideologically conditioned, even with respect to the knowledge it asserts to have of the world. Religion, of course, has long had to suffer such attacks and the impugning of its claimed knowledge of God and humanity. The presuppositions of what I say here will be 'critically realist' with respect to both science and theology. That is to say, I think that both science and theology *aim* to depict reality; that they both do so in metaphorical language with the use of models; and that their metaphors and models are revisable within the context of the continuous communities which have generated them.

This philosophy of *science* has the virtue of being the implicit, though often not articulated, working philosophy of practising scientists who aim to depict reality but know only too well their fallibility in doing so. A formidable case for such a critical scientific realism has, in my view, been mounted[116] based on the histories of, for example, of geology, cell biology and chemistry, which during the last two centuries have progressively uncovered hidden structures in the entities of the natural world that account causally for observed phenomena. Note that this view asserts only that it is the *aim* of science to depict reality as best it may – it is, rather, a programme for the natural sciences. Models and metaphors are widely used in science but this does not detract from the aim of such language to refer to realities while it does entail that these models and metaphors are always in principle revisable.

Now *theology*, the intellectual formulation of religious beliefs and explication of religious experience employs models which may be similarly described.[117] I urge[118] that a critical realism is also the most appropriate and adequate philosophy concerning religious language and theological propositions: theological concepts and models should be regarded as partial, inadequate and revisable, but necessary and, indeed, the only ways of referring to the reality that is named as 'God' and to God's relation with humanity. Models and metaphors play an even more obvious role in religious language then in science. Theology should also be attempting to infer to the best explanation by application of the normal criteria of reasonableness: fit with the data, internal coherence, comprehensiveness, fruitfulness and general cogency.[119]

It is the aim of theology to tell as true a story as possible. Like science, it too must allow graduations in the degree of acceptance, in the belief in the 'truth', of theological propositions and must recognise that there is a hierarchy of truths – some more focal and central (and defensible) than others. The whole theological enterprise has often been criticized because it has been said to have no way comparable in rigour to that of science the sifting and testing of its 'data' – in this case, the content of religious experience and tradition and the scriptures that preserve some of them. However, some philosophers of religion have in fact been able to mount what seems to me to be an effective defence of the warranty of religious belief as expressed theologically.[120] For theology, like science, also attempts to make inferences to the best explanation – or, rather, it should be attempting to do so. In order to do this it should use the criteria of reasonableness already mentioned, for these are criteria which at least have the potentiality of leading to agreement between people of different traditions (even within Christianity). Some signs that this might not be an entirely forlorn hope are provided by the changes that were at least initiated in the Roman Catholic Church by Vatican II; by the development during this century of the World Council of (non-Roman) Churches and by the dialogue between the world's major religions which is really only just beginning.

The need now is for theology to develop the application of its criteria of reasonableness in a community in which no authority would be automatic (for example, of the form 'the Church says, the Bible says' – for all such arguements are circular). Truths that are claimed to be revealed or are the promulgations of ecclesiastical authority cannot avoid running the gauntlet of these criteria of reasonableness, for they cannot be at the same time both self-warranting and convincing. This approach needs to be combined with an openness to development as human knowledge expands and experience is further enriched. When I urge this kind of critically realist aim and programme on Christians, and indeed on the adherents of all religions, I cannot help feeling a little like William Temple[121] who is reputed to have said: 'I pray daily for Christ's one holy, catholic and apostolic Church – and that it may yet come into existence'. That could also be said of the present situation of a critical-realist theology. It has broadly the same intentions as that described by Hans Küng[122], namely 'truthful', 'free', 'critical', and 'ecumenical' – a theology which deals with and interprets the realities of all that constitutes the world, especially human beings and our own inner selves.

In spite of what the 'cultured despisers' of Christianity might say, there *are* 'data' available to the theological enterprise, just as there are to the scientific. They are constituted by the religious experience of those in the well-winnowed traditions of the major world religions, among them Christianity, which provides our principal source in the West of tested wisdom about how to refer to that which is encountered in those experiences initially dubbed as experiences of God. In this perspective both science and theology are engaged with realities that may be referred to and it is therefore entirely appropriate to ask how what scientists believe about the natural world and religious people believe about God and human nature might, or should, be related – as they always have been historically.

What is the vista that twentieth-century science unveils for our contemplation? We know now that we live in a world that, extrapolating backwards in our clock time, may be said to have 'begun' some 10 or so billion years ago in the fluctuation of a quantum field which became an unimaginably condensed mass of fundamental particles and quanta of energy that has over millions of years coalesced, in an expanding space, into the present observable universe, with its billion galaxies each containing between a hundred and a hundred thousand million stars. On one planet near one of these stars – our Earth – in one of these galaxies, the composition, temperature and age were such as to allow the formation of more and more complex molecules from the atoms it had inherited from some supernovae explosion aeons before. By their inherent properties some systems of molecules came into existence that could copy their own patterns of organization – matter then became living. The forms of living matter expanded by the incorporation into their systems of other molecules and in doing so competed with each other for limited resources. Those life forms that produced the most copies of themselves at a greater rate persisted longer than others – the evolution of living organisms by natural selection was under way. The advantage of acquiring new functions and abilities in response to changing conditions of climate and predations of other living organisms stimulated an increase in complexity as time proceeded. We note that the history of the cosmos and of life on the Earth manifests an emergent quality – for the concepts which are hammered out by the sciences appropriate to each level of complexity, and which are needed to describe and account for specific systems, cannot be reduced to those that are pertinent to their constituents. Genuinely new kinds of reality appear in the evolutionary process in the course of time.

The advantages of accurate information-processing systems to predict and adjust to environmental changes induced the development of sensitive monitoring and information-storing systems – in fact, sense, nerves and brains. This advantage could be further compounded by social communication and organization – thus language, and so forms of consciousness, emerged under pressures of natural selection in those creatures capable of such information retrieval. These propensities – towards complexity, self-organisation, information-processing and consciousness – eventually coalesced in the uniquely concentrated form of the personal self-consciousness of *homo sapiens* who – be it noted – might have exemplified the embodiment of these propensities in a quite different physical form, such is the interplay of chance of law, of sheer happenstance, in the evolutionary process. Thus the original fluctuation in a quantum field has taken the form of human persons with all their creativity and diversity.

The humanity which has thus come into existence through this seamless web of evolutionary natural processes, as now unveiled in broad outline by the sciences, seeks urgently and even passionately for the meaning of its own existence and of that from which and within which it has emerged. This long search for meaning is the religious quest of humanity. It cannot but be affected by this new perspective from the sciences of where we have come from and the processes that have resulted in us being here at all. This is the broad challenge of science to religion – and indeed to all human reflection on our nature and destiny.

So let us look at some of the challenges to certain central themes in Christian belief and consider what revisions of inherited images and metaphors might be the best way to respond to them.

God
The primary attribute of God in the monotheistic religions is that

of 'transcendence' over all-that-is – that God has a distinct mode of being from everything else. This is based on the sound instinct that the existence of all-that-is is not-explanatory. Even the original quantum fluctuation, from which our observable universe is currently thought to have expanded, had to have a mode of being of a kind to which quantum mechanics could specifically apply, so that it had to be a fluctuation in a 'field' of a kind describable by the laws of that science. It was not just 'nothing at all' even if it was 'no *thing*'! The affirmation of the existence and transcendence of God is, then, a response to the question 'Why is there anything at all?', a response to the sheer givenness of it all – and the need for such a response is enhanced by the scientifically perceived subtlety and rationality of the observed universe.

This response involves the recognition of God as Creator, who gives being to all-that-is; of God as the ground of all being, Being itself; and of the world as having a derived and dependent existence. This constitutes one of the fundamental pillars of Christian theology, indeed of all the monotheistic religions.

The givenness of the parameters of the universe have been brought sharply into focus recently in that cluster of physical considerations which is referred to as the 'anthropic principle' – the fact that this universe is characterized by a particular set of laws and fundamental constants which prove to be just those that could allow the development of living matter, of life, and so of ourselves. It re-emphasizes, firstly, what in the monotheistic religions of the world is perceived as the contingency of all-that-is. Everything could have been otherwise; it need not have been at all in the form it now has. Hence it gives new grounds for recognising the contingency of our own existence and so of God's transcendence – though I myself am less sure that it actually constitutes an argument for the existence of God. Secondly, it restores for our generation a sense of how integrated our human existence is with the physical cosmos, that cosmos whose sheer scale seems, on our first apprehension of it, so daunting, threatening even. Not only is this earth our natural home – so is this universe!

In twentieth-century physics there has been a development, initiated by Einstein, in which the categories of space and time, which seemed so given and *a priori* to Kant – and to 'common' sense – are themselves interlocked with each other in a new kind of relation. For space, time, matter and energy have become mutually defined concepts which modern physicists link closely together. This challenges naïve understandings of the doctrine of creation. For any notion that God gives being to all-that-is, must now include time as an aspect of, a real relation within, what God has created, as St Augustine well knew. Our understanding of the doctrine of creation is restored to what the profoundest thinkers in the monotheistic religions have always affirmed: that it is not a statement about what happened 'in' space and time, for space-time, matter and energy are all aspects of the created order. God has to be regarded as other than, and transcending, the space-time, matter and energy of the physicists. The doctrine of creation is fundamentally about the *relation* of God to all-that-is, and this includes space-time-matter-energy. It is not at all about what happened at 4004 BC or even 10 billion BC!

However, with the biblical authors, Christians and Jews believe that God is not entirely 'timeless'. For they all regard God as, in some sense, 'personal' – at least misleadingly described by personal metaphors, as interacting with human beings in a way best understood as like personal relationships. So God is pictured as experiencing a sense of succession in relation to the world, including human beings. We cannot put God, as it were, on a mountain top from which God views all time – past, present and future – and thus foresees all future events (including those involving ourselves) for that limits, indeed destroys, our freedom. For us to be free, God cannot know certainly what we will decide. There is no simple fact of the matter ('At 10.30 a.m. tomorrow, I will do X ...') for even an omniscient God, or for us, to know. I would suggest that we can best think of God giving existence to all-that-is, i.e., creating moment by moment, each interval of that relation we call physical time (in our particular relativistic frame-work) – which is what the traditional notion of God sustaining and preserving matter-energy in space-time must now be taken to signify. That is how I, and some others, respond to the challenge of the modern physical understanding of space-time-matter-energy in relation to the idea of God as Creator.[123]

The scientific perspective also challenges, and I think enriches, our notion of another classical attribute of God in the monotheistic religions, namely the presence of God *in* the world, the 'immanence' of God. We observe, through the sciences, the operation of natural processes that are continuously and inherently creative, for matter has the ability to be self-organizing into new forms. The process is open-ended and the details of the processes are often unpredictable by us − either because of in-principle 'Heisenberg' uncertainty at the sub-atomic level, or because of the in-practice inevitable, unpredictability of the future states of certain, far from uncommon, non-linear macroscopic systems. There seems to be an in-built tendency in matter, and the processes it undergoes, towards complexity, self-organization, information transfer, and ultimately, consciousness, cognition and self-consciousness. Potentialities appear to be being actualized. The original 'hot big bang', with its cloud of neutrinos, quarks or whatever, has becomes *us*. Nature not only has, but *is* a history of events. There seems to be no inert stuff in the universe, for all entities and structures are in dynamic process in which the universe manifests emergence of the genuinely new. *New* realities go on appearing.

If we are to think of God as Creator of such a universe, then we are bound to re-emphasize that God is still creat*ing* in, with and under the processes of the natural world all the time. God is all the time the Creator − it is an ongoing, continuous relation. God as Creator not only, in this perspective, sustains and preserves the world (the traditional understanding) but must now be regarded as continuously creating in, with and under these creative processes. In unveiling the natural processes whereby new forms come into existence, science is revealing God at work as Creator. God has now to be understood as, as it were, 'exploring' and actualizing the potentialities of creation, achieving ends flexibly without laying down determinate lines in advance. God is improvising rather as did J. S. Bach before the King of Prussia or perhaps like an extemporizing New Orleans jazz player in Preservation Hall. Creation is the action of God-the-Composer-and-Improviser at work.

Moreover, in some sense, the world is in God, yet God is more than the world. God gives new forms and life to what is in God, in 'God herself', we find ourselves having to say. God is present to all-that-is, the circumambient Reality that flows in and around all, Creator-Mother as much as Creator-Father.

Strangely enough, science affords some new perspectives on the perennial mysteries of death, pain and suffering. For, through our scientific spectacles, we now know that death of the individual is the pre-condition of the evolving by natural selection of new life, and new forms of life. Furthermore, consciousness, and so awareness, cannot evolve without the development of nervous systems and sensitive recording organs which inevitably have to be able to react negatively to dangers in their environment with what we call pain. It appears that pain and its corollary, suffering, in conscious beings are the pre-conditions of sensitivity, consciousness and self-consciousness. What religious thinkers used to call 'natural evil' now appears in a new light as a necessary part of a universe capable of generating new forms of life and consciousness. This has the implication that, for our notion of God to be at all morally acceptable, we have to regard Godself as suffering in, with and under the creative processes of the world – a perception now widely accepted by many Christian thinkers. God is, then, to be conceived as suffering and enduring what we call natural evil for achieving the ultimate good and fruition of what is being created namely, *inter alia*, free-willing, self-conscious persons.

God and the world
But now we have to face another apparent challenge from the sciences to religious thinking. How can we think of God interacting with, and possibly influencing, events in a world in which all its processes and events are increasingly rendered lawlike and intelligible by the sciences, which include those of the brain sciences and psychology? How can God affect events, or patterns of events, in the world now made manifest by the sciences, without disrupting its very God-given regularities at its various levels of complexity. Many in the past have been driven to think of God as some kind of *deus ex machina* who, from some lofty transcendent throne, intervenes in the very fabric of the causal network

which that same God is regarded as having created. Oddly enough, science, in explicating aspects of what personal agency might be, now also helps us to clarify how God might be conceived to interact with the world and influence events without breaking the very regularities that Godself has created.

In the perspective of the sciences human beings are seen as psychosomatic unities, evolving by natural processes, emerging into consciousness and self-consciousness. Biblical scholars also emphasize that this non-dualist view of the human being as a psychosomatic unity is indeed that of the Old Testament and also underlies that of the New. This can give us an important clue to making more intelligible the belief that God interacts with the world to make some things happen rather than others. When we act, total brain states, which we experience subjectively as thoughts, intentions, purposes, etc., are causally effective in the many-tiered levels of our bodies. This action of our brain-in-our-bodies is a holistic one, in the top-down direction and what happens at the 'lower' levels is entirely consistent with the known regularities of muscle biochemistry, physiology, neurology, etc. This is but one of the more significant, proposed, examples (also in biochemistry, chemistry, physics, etc.) of the way in which the *state* of a whole macroscopic complex system affects and constrains the events occurring at the micro-level of its constituent parts – a kind of whole-part constraint (or 'top-down causation', as it has less felicitously been called).

Such systems suggest a model for how God might be conceived of as interacting with the world – for how God might be causally effective in a whole-part relationship which does not abrogate the known regularities of events at their own distinctive level of description by the appropriate sciences. This would not be an 'intervening' God, but would be a God *continuously* interacting with the totality of the world, shaping through God's own constraint upon the whole both the general course of events and the patterns of particular ones.[124] God is faithful to the order of God's own creation and does not act in a way inconsistent with its God-created regularities. Moreover we now see that God has let God's own acts be circumscribed by the character of the natural order Godself has created, even including the inherent unpredictability of events at the Heisenberg level and of those macroscopic events which result, in some cases, from amplification of quantum ones.

This implies that the model of personal agency is still fruitful in helping us to conceive of God's interaction with the world. But now it is enriched and nuanced by new insights into the brain-body relation, into whole-part constraint in complex systems and into the openness and flexibility inherent in the natural world.

Humanity

Like all living organisms, human beings have a finite life and we have come to recognize through the scientific understanding of evolution the biological necessity of the death of the individual. We as individuals would not be here at all, as members of the species *homo sapiens* if our forerunners in the evolutionary process had not died. Biological death was present on the earth long before human beings arrived on the scene and is the pre-requisite of our coming into existence through the processes of biological evolution whereby God creates new species, including ourselves. So when St Paul says that 'sin pays a wage, and the wage is death'[125] that cannot possibly mean for us now *biological* death and can only mean 'death' in some other sense, such as the death of our relation to God consequent upon sin. I can see no sense in regarding biological death as the consequence of that very real alienation from God that is sin, because God had already used biological death as the means for creating new forms of life, subsequently including ourselves, long before we appeared on the Earth. This means those classical Christian formulations of the theology of the redemptive work of Christ that assume a causal connection between biological death and sin urgently need revising.

Moreover, the scientific evidence is that human nature has emerged only gradually by a continuous process from earlier hominids and there are no sudden breaks of any substantial kind in the sequences noted by palaeontologists and anthropologists. There is no past period for which there is evidence that human beings possessed moral perfection existing in a paradisal situation from which there has been only subsequent decline. All the evidence points to a creature slowly emerging into awareness, with an increasing capacity for consciousness and sensitivity and the possibility of moral responsibility and, the religions would affirm, of response to God. So there is no sense in which we can talk of a 'Fall' from a past perfection. There was no golden age, no perfect past, no original perfect, individual 'Adam' from whom all human beings have now declined. What *is* true is that humanity manifests aspirations to a perfection not yet attained, a potentiality not yet actualized, but no 'original righteousness'. Sin as alienation from God, humanity and nature is real and is about a falling short of what God intends us to be and is concomitant with our possession of self-consciousness, freedom and intellectual curiosity. The classical conceptions of the 'Fall' and of 'sin' that dominate Christian theologies of redemption urgently need, it seems to me, re-casting if they are to make any sense to our contemporaries.

The questions of not only 'Who are we?' but, even more acutely, 'What should we be becoming – where should we be going?' remain acute for us. If the clue to the answers to these questions lies in the person of Jesus of Nazareth (as I shall maintain), we have to ask.

Who is Jesus?
– viewed against the backcloth of the vista of cosmological and biological evolution that the sciences now give us.

Since AD 451, the Definition of Chalcedon has been taken as the criterion of orthodoxy. It affirmed that Jesus was 'complete in regard to his humanity', that is, 'completely human' – indeed 'perfect' in the sense of 'complete' (John Robinson[126]) – fully human, but (note) *not* necessarily displaying perfection in all conceivable human characteristics. Any assessment of Jesus must start here, along with recognizing his special vocation and relation to God.

But, one may well ask, is not this starting point in Jesus undoubted humanity called into question by the assertion in the traditions about Jesus that there were acts of his and events associated with him that have a supposedly supernatural connotation: the reported 'miracles'? If by a 'miracle', one means an event interpreted as not fully explicable by naturalistic means, then judgement must depend on one's *a priori* attitudes towards the very possibility of such events occurring in principle – and a scientific age is, in my view, properly sceptical, demanding very much stronger historical evidence for them than for ordinary ones – and this is not usually forthcoming. Briefly, I consider[127] that in general the healings and apparent exorcisms give rise to no special difficulties (even a scientific age recognizes the psychosomatic basis of health), but that the 'nature miracles' certainly do so; and moreover that these latter usually have features that either denote them as pure legend or as stories told with an overload of symbolic meanings – in fact, true 'myths'!

More pertinent to our theme are the major 'miracles' connected with the person of Jesus himself.[128] Firstly, as regards the birth narratives, the conclusion of the cautious – and very thorough – Roman Catholic scholar, Raymond Brown, is worth quoting: 'the *scientifically controllable* biblical evidence leaves the question of the historicity of the virginal conception unresolved.'[129] This verdict would be regarded as over-cautious by other scholars less restrained by an ecclesiastical *magisterium*. John Macquarrie indeed affirms that '... our historical information is negligible ... apart from scraps of doubtful information, the birth narratives [of Matthew and Luke] are manifestly legendary in character.'[130]

Biological science, in fact, also raises acute questions about the 'Virginal Conception' . Since females possess only X chromosomes, conception without a father to provide a Y chromosome could lead only to a female child with two XX chromosomes – unless there was some kind of divine *de novo* creation of a Y chromosome in the ovum entering Mary's uterus – for the birth narratives in the Gospels never deny, and indeed affirm, a normal gestation period of nine months. Even such a miraculous, almost magical, act would be beset with problems – what genes should the DNA of this Y chromosome possess? – those to give similarities to Joseph, or, if not, of whom? So one can go on piling Ossa on Pelion.

But a more general consideration now weighs heavily because of its theological import. If Jesus is really to be fully and completely human, all that we now know scientifically about human nature shows that he must share both our evolutionary history and have the same multi-levelled, including genetic, basis for his personhood – and that means he must be not only flesh of our flesh and bone of our bone, but also DNA of our DNA. If he does not, to use the traditional terms, our salvation is in jeopardy for 'what he has not assumed he has not healed'[131]. Hence it is theologically imperative that the birth stories and the doctrine of the virginal conception of Jesus be separated from the doctrine of the incarnation and be regarded in the same light as those about Adam and Eve – that is, as mythical and legendary stories intending to convey non-historical and non-biological truths. In this instance the truth includes the assertion that God took the initiative in shaping and creating the person and life of Jesus of Nazareth.[132]

The situation is quite otherwise with that other major, postulated 'miracle' concerning the person of Jesus – that complex of events we call his Resurrection (and in which I will include also the Ascension or Exaltation). It is not at all clear that the narratives, as such, of the Resurrection are sensitive to scientific considerations at all, since the end state, the 'risen' Jesus is not open even to the kind of repeatable observations science and indeed ordinary experience involves. The historical evidence is that this was a genuine experience within the consciousness of these witnesses. Such a complex of experiences, especially when they are communal, could well manifest a new reality only discernible in that particular complex combination. For the concept of 'resurrection' appears not to be reducible to any purely psychological account and the affirmations of the New Testament can properly be claimed to be referring to a new kind of reality hitherto unknown because not hitherto experienced – and on which the sciences as such can make no comment. I recall the penetrating statement of Christopher Evans:

> 'The core of resurrection faith is that already within the temporal order of existence a new beginning of life from God, and a living of life under God, are possible, and are anticipatory of what human life has it in it to be as divine creation; and that this has been made apprehensible and

available in the life and death of Christ regarded both as
divine illumination of human life and as effective power for
overcoming whatever obstructs it.'[133]

Jesus' resurrection demonstrated to the disciples, notably to Paul,
and now to us, that it is the union of his kind of life with God
which is not broken by death and capable of being taken up into
God. For he manifested the kind of human life which can become
not only fully life with God, here and now, but eternally beyond
the threshold of death. Hence his imperative 'Follow me' now
constitutes for us a call for the transformation of humanity into a
new kind of human being and becoming. What happened to him,
Jesus, *could* happen to all.

   In this perspective, Jesus the Christ, the whole Christ event, has
shown us what is possible for humanity. The actualization of this
potentiality can properly be regarded as the consummation of the
purposes of God in the evolution of humanity. In Jesus there was
a divine act of new creation because the initiative was from God
within human history, within the responsive human will of Jesus
inspired by that outreach of God into humanity traditionally
designated as 'God the Holy Spirit'. Jesus the Christ is thereby
seen, in the context of the whole complex of events in which he
participated (the 'Christ event'), as the paradigm, indeed paragon,
of what God intends for all human beings, now revealed as having
the potentiality of responding to, of being open to, of becoming
united with, God.

   But how can what happened in and to him be effectual today
after two millennia in a way that might actually change us so that
we live in harmony with God, ourselves and our fellow human
beings? This to consider what has traditionally been called

The work of Christ

I can here only sketchily outline how such questions might be
answered.[134] Any answer to be credible today will have to be
grounded on our sharing a common humanity with this Jesus.
There are certain features in the scientific perspectives we have
been delineating which now properly constrain this response,
namely:

- biological death of the individual, as the means of the evolutionary creation of new species by natural selection, present in the world aeons before human being appeared, cannot now be attributed to human sin; and
- the evidence is all against human beings ever in the past having been in some golden age of innocence and perfection from which they have 'fallen'.

The Nicene Creed simply affirms that Christ 'was crucified *for us* under Pontius Pilate. He suffered and was buried'. This reticent 'for us' encompasses a very wide range of interpretations. Although the church in its many branches has never officially endorsed any one particular theory of this claimed at-one-ment, yet a number have become widely disseminated doctrinally, liturgically and devotionally. They all (with the exception of that of Abelard) propose a change in God's relation and attitudes to humanity because of Jesus' death on the cross. These purportedly 'objective' theories of the atonement also rely heavily on presuppositions contrary to the two features of human history mentioned above which are based on well-founded science. Moreover, they also fail to incorporate our sense, derived from the vista of evolution unfolded by the sciences, of humanity as *emerging* in a process into individual and corporate consciousness and self-consciousness, awareness of values, social co-operation, human culture; and into a sense of and awareness of God. The classical theories of the atonement fail to express any dynamic sense of the process of human *becoming* as still going on. They also fail to make clear how the human response which is an essential part of the reconciliation between God and humanity is evoked.

So let us now put the question again as: How can what happened in and to Jesus the Christ actually evoke in us the response that is needed for our reconciliation to God and actually enable us to live in harmony with God and humanity here and now? This question may be answered most effectively, it seems to me, by seeing the life, suffering and death of Jesus the Christ as an act of love: an act of love *of* God, an act of love *by* God.

In the suffering and death of Jesus the Christ, we now also concomitantly perceive and experience the suffering, self-offering love of God in action, no more as abstract knowledge, but actually in the flesh. For the openness and obedience of the human Jesus to God enabled him, as *the* God-informed human person, to be a manifest self-expression in history, in the confines of human personhood, of God as creative self-expressing Word/*Logos*/'Son'. Thereby is uniquely and definitively revealed the depths of the divine Love for humanity and the cost of God's gracious outreach to us as we are, alienated from God, humanity and ourselves, that is, as 'sinners'. As such, this love of God engages us, where 'to engage' means (OED): 'to attract and hold fast; to involve; to lay under obligation; to urge, induce' to gain, win over'. The Cross is a proposal of God's love and as such engages our response. Once we have really come to know that it was God's love in action 'for us' which was manifest in the self-offering love and obedience of Jesus the Christ, then we can never be the same again. God in that outreach to humanity, we denote as God the Holy Spirit, united the human Jesus with God's own self and can now kindle and generate in us a love for God and for the humanity for whom Jesus dies, as we contemplate God in Christ on the cross.

What I am proposing here is that this action of God as Holy Spirit in us engages our response and this itself effects our at-one-ment, is itself salvific, actually making us whole, making us 'holier'. Such an understanding of the 'work of Christ' coheres with our present evolutionary perceptions that the specifically human emerged and still emerges only gradually and fitfully in human history, without a historic 'Fall'.

For since God took Jesus through death into his own life, it is implicit in this initiation and continuation of this process in us, that we too can thereby be taken up into the life of God, can be 'resurrected' in some way akin to that of Jesus the Christ. Since Jesus was apprehended as having been taken through death with his personhood and identity intact and as having been 'taken up' into the presence of God, it could happen to us and that is the ground of our hope for our individual future and that of humanity corporately.[135]

Furthermore the interpretation of the death and resurrection of Jesus as manifesting uniquely the quality of life that can be taken

up by God into the fullness of God's own life implicitly involves
an affirmation about what the basic potentiality of all humanity is.
It shows us that, regardless of our particular human skills and
creativities – indeed regardless of almost all that the social mores
of our times applauds – it is through a radical openness to God, a
thoroughgoing self-offering love for others and obedience to God
that we grow into such communion with the external God that
God does not allow biological death to rupture that potentially
timeless relation. Irenaeus says it all: 'The Word of God, Our
Lord Jesus Christ, who of his boundless love became what we are
to make us what even he himself is.'[136]

Conclusion

If the foregoing has any weight then it is an example of the way
that the Church might re-state its message in today's language for
a society deeply impressed by and indebted to science. The old
images, although they may still be evocative and meaningful for
those steeped in traditional language, no longer appear at all
credible to those outside the churches and other religious
institutions, which is 90% of those in the United Kingdom and
most of Europe, it seems from all the surveys. We need a
rebirth of images in continuity with what we have inherited from
the classical scriptures and traditions; we need to revise how
we speak to the eternal realities to which the Christian faith seeks
to refer.

The importance of ideas, both in the short and the long run,
cannot be overestimated. Those members of the Church who take
no account of the scientific picture of the world are forfeiting the
future viability of the good news for humanity that is in Jesus the
Christ. They are digging themselves into a deeper and deeper hole
and, as they go down, they will be able to talk more and more to
themselves and less and less to other thinking people. For in
God's good time, truth will out.

26

Religio Philosophi Naturalis
(The religion of a scientist)

'The wisdome of God receives small honour from those
vulgar heads, that rudely stare about, and with a grosse
rusticity admire his workes; those highly magnifie him
whose judicious enquiry into his acts, and deliberate
research into his creatures, returne the duty of a devout
and learned admiration.'
Sir Thomas Browne (Religio Medici, 1643).[137]

Sir Thomas Browne and his 'Religio Medici'

In 1671, King Charles II on his visit to the city of Norwich, in
Norfolk, East Anglia, with his usual largesse decided to confer a
knighthood on the city's mayor but, the latter declining (for
reasons unknown), he then bestowed it on the local doctor, one
Thomas Browne, who had then lived there for more than half of
his life. Adventitious as this event was, the royal visitor could
scarcely have given this honour more judiciously. For Sir Thomas
Browne, as we must now call him, was not only a physician –
with the best degrees of his time from Oxford and Leyden, and a
former student at Montpelier and Padua – but he was also a man
of prodigious and catholic learning in at least nine languages,
natural philosophy (the sciences we would call them), literature,
practical arts, and much more – his various tracts are concerned
with more than 27 different fields of study.

But, above all, he was a devout and informed Christian, curious
in his faith, eirenical, tolerant and (we would say) ecumenical in
his disposition in times when such attitudes were rare in a land
only recently torn by civil war and revolution over religious as
well as political ideologies. He himself was, as he tells us in his
most important work, the *Religio Medici*, of the 'reformed, new-
cast Religion, wherein I dislike nothing but the name [of

Protestant], of the same belief our Saviour taught, the Apostles disseminated, the Fathers authorised, and the Martyrs confirmed'. (p. 61).[138] For, he tells us later, referring to *Roman* Catholics, 'we have reformed from them, not against them' (p. 62), and goes on to express his broad tolerance of those practices and beliefs of theirs which he preferred not to adopt.

But what he is most remembered for is his rhythmic and subtle prose writings which remain a jewel in the crown that is rightly conferred on the English language of his century – he was, for example, enthusiastically adopted as a model by Hermann Melville in *Moby Dick*. His most influential work is that already mentioned, *Religio Medici*, the 'Religion of a Doctor'. In that work, he stands at the watershed between medieval perceptions of nature, humanity and God and those of the new 'natural philosophy', the programme – as we might say – of that Royal Society of London founded during his lifetime.

Many of us today intuit that we too, in the last decade of this century, are also traversing, indeed have already traversed, a watershed not dissimilar from the one he was crossing, that between a culture in which religion is at least taken seriously to one in which science alone is listened to. It is worth looking a little more closely at Sir Thomas Browne's all-inclusive vista for it has features we can recognize as germain to ourselves.

For him, there were vertical and horizontal dimensions to existence which he combined in a cosmic and transcendent unity through the use of reason in the form of a ' "Divine Sagacity" … the dynamic power of the mind to encompass "the close connexion and cohesion" of the diverse aspects of the universe' (p. 26).[139] The vertical dimension in his thought was the Scale of Nature which he described thus: '… there is in this Universe a Staire, or manifest Scale of creatures, rising not disorderly, or in confusion, but with a comely method and proportion' (p. 101). This hierarchical view of his was one he shared with his contemporaries, of levels of existence in a system of analogies and correspondences from the least plant to the very angels. Ours, we shall see, is rather one of structures, entities and processes; of methodologies and of concepts. Furthermore, we could perhaps also enrich our disclosure by use of two of his favourite metaphors.

One is that of music which, he says, 'strikes in mee a deepe fit of devotion, and a profound contemplation of the first Composer, there is something in it of Divinity more than the eare discovers … it is a sensible fit of that Harmony, which intellectually sounds in the eares of God' (p. 149–150). The other is that of the circle as symbolic of the omnipresence of God 'whose center is everywhere, and circumference no where' (p. 450, quoted from another of Browne's works, *Christian Morals*).

Browne also discerned cosmic unity in the horizontal dimension of historical process which he identified, like his contemporaries, with the broadly biblical, Judeo-Christian view of history as expressing the divine purpose from the Creation to the Last Judgement. For him, 'the created World is but a small *Parenthesis* in Eternity' (p. 471, also in *Christian Morals*) and there was for him a profound contrast between the processes of time which we can hope to understand, and that of divine Eternal Present, which we cannot. Our culture too, it must be noted, even when it does not share that perspective, has its horizontal dimension in our perception of cosmic and biological evolution.

So presented, through the prejudiced and distorting lens of my own undoubted attraction to the man and his thought, perhaps you can agree that Sir Thomas Browne develops themes which might perhaps find at least an echo in the religion of a late-twentieth century scientist, a *religo philosophi naturalis* for today. But the waters of three centuries of natural philosophy, of the natural and human sciences, have gone under the bridge since his day and we now face new challenges – not least those also coming from historical criticism of the Bible and of other sources of authority for earlier times. These have removed many of the pillars on which his world, and even that of the previous century, have been constructed. Browne wrote from his position as a life-time Christian believer, reflecting on the world he knew, not least as a doctor, and relying – though not totally uncritically – on ancient authorities.

A scientist encounters nature and is led to theistic inferences
But my own experience of the Christian religion[140] as a *scientist* has to begin with the time when I first began actually to *do*

science. This occurred only when I was, after a lengthy apprenticeship, actually posing questions to 'Nature', by putting her, as it were, to the test of experiments of my own devising and execution. By that time I had become sceptical and agnostic about the beliefs of that same English reformed, catholic Christianity to which Browne has adhered, no longer 'new-cast' as it appeared freshly to him and thereby, no doubt, less appealing three centuries later to someone also in their twenties as I then was (only just a little younger than when Browne wrote the *Religio Medici*).

Doing research as a graduate student, questions kept pressing on me. How *could* one explain and account for what every scientific advance unveiled and reinforced, namely the inherent, if hidden, intelligibility and rationality of the natural world? As Einstein famously expressed it: 'The eternal mystery of the world is its comprehensibiliy'[141] Both the *fact* of its existence (the question 'Why is there anything all?') and its manifest rationality seemed to demand some kind of theistic affirmation to make any coherent sense of it all – and asking 'Why?' and making sense of a wide range of data was just what my training and research experience were making my habitual practice.

That there is anything at all implies the existence of some ground of being and becoming other than the world and its inherent rationality suggests further that such a Ground must be supra-rational in the sense of being able to give existence to a world embodying rationality. There have been many names for this Ground in different religions but in English the name was and is 'God', as long as we recognize that *ex hypothesi* we can never in principle know the nature of God in God's own self and that we will always have to refer to God by analogy, metaphor and model. So this was but the beginning of my pilgrimage as a scientist seeking to make coherent sense of the world in all its aspects.

I have already described some of my steps along that way[142] and the various signposts other than the sciences which pointed me along it. I shall continue here mainly with the scientific considerations that I found relevant to my own religious quest.

An initial encounter, via DNA, with emergence
– and with reductionism

As it happened, when I had completed my apprenticeship and was pursuing research entirely of my own devising, in my first university post, it was mainly centred on what we now call DNA. In the late 1940s and early 1950s DNA has been identified as the principle carrier of the genes but it was still not certain even that it was a large molecule – and, of course, although it was known to contain nucleotides linked together in chains of uncertain length, its double-helical structure was unknown. I forbear here from regaling you with my own personal recollections and anecdotes of the complex choreography executed by the principle characters involved in the unveiling of its double-helical structure. Suffice to say that it revolutionized biology and has now become part of the public awareness of the world. What gradually especially impressed itself on me – and it is a clue to many important issues in the epistemology and relationships of the sciences – is that for the first time we were witnessing the existence of a complex macromolecule the chemical structure of which had the ability to convey information, the genetic instructions to the next generation to be like its parent(s). Now the concept of 'information', originating in the mathematical theory of communication (C. E. Shannon), had never been part of the organic chemistry of nucleotides, even of polynucleotides. Hence in DNA we were witnessing a notable example of what many reflecting on the evolutionary process have called 'emergence' – the entirely neutral name[143] for the general feature of natural process – wherein complex structures, especially in living organisms, develop distinctively new capabilities and functions at levels of greater complexity. Such emergence is an undoubted, observed feature of the evolutionary process, especially of the biological. It was eventually for me the goad that stimulated to wider reflections, firstly, epistemological, on the relations among the bodies of knowledge which different sciences provide; and, secondly, ontological, on the nature of the realities which the sciences putatively claim to disclose.

Francis Crick, one of the discoverers of the DNA structure, for which he shared the Nobel Prize with another Englishman,

Maurice Wilkins and the American, James Watson, early threw
down the gauntlet in these matters by declaring that 'the ultimate
aim of the modern movement in biology is in fact to explain *all*
biology in terms of physics and chemistry'.[144] Such a challenge
can, in fact, be mounted at many other interfaces between the
sciences other than that between biology and physics/chemistry.
We have all witnessed the attempted takeover bids, for example,
of psychology by neurophysiology and of anthropology and sociology by biology. The game is that of 'reductionism' or, more
colloquially, 'nothing-buttery' – 'discipline X (usually meaning
yours) is really nothing but discipline Y (which happens to be
mine).' (So – the hidden agenda – that is the direction the grants
should go too?)

Reductionism again; and the map of knowledge
– scientific and humanistic
It became clear to me over the years that the issues involved in
such reductionist claims are significant not only in relation to in-
fighting between the sciences, or rather between scientists, but for
our apprehension of the whole map of knowledge, including the
status of the humanities and of theology, the intellectual articulation of religious experience and traditions. Figure 1[145] represents
the relation between the different focal levels of interest and of
analysis of the various sciences, especially as they pertain to
human beings, rather like the different levels of resolution of a
microscope.

The scheme represented is an epistemological one concerned
with the foci of interest, and so of analysis, that naturally arise
from the, quite properly, methodologically reductionist techniques of the sciences – the necessary breaking down of complex
wholes into their smaller units for investigation. The figure illustrates 'part-whole' hierarchies of complexity in which the science
focusing on the more complex 'wholes' are distinct from those
focusing on the parts that constitute them. Such relations occur
both horizontally, within the four broad categories of the boxes,
and vertically, though it is these latter which are of most concern
to us now. For, as one goes up the figure, one finds the need to
deploy distinctively new concepts and theories containing new

referential terms in order to represent the observed capacities and functions and to describe accurately the structures, entities and processes which occur at those more complex levels (inevitably 'higher' on the printed page).

Such considerations eventually led me to go into the subtle and sometimes raging, debate concerning reductionism, provoked first among biologists by Crick's remarks and later among anthropologists and sociologists by E. O. Wilson, the sociobiologist. Briefly stated, I concluded that in many important instances the concepts and theories that constitute the content of the sciences focusing on the more complex levels are often (not always) logically not reducible to those operative in the sciences that focus on their components. Sometimes a variety of independent derivation, identification, or measurement procedures directed at a particular complex level find an invariance in the concepts and referential terms of the theories needed to account for the phenomena associated with them. W. C. Wimsatt[146] of the University of Chicago has called these 'robust', for what is yielded by the procedures appropriate to each level of investigation can then be said to be real, if only in the pragmatic sense that we cannot avoid taking account of them in our dealings and interactions with them. In such instances, there is a prima facie case that the concepts and deferential terms of the theories deployed in relation to the more complex levels actually refer to new realities distinctively emerging at those levels of complexity. There is then an emergence which could be said to be 'ontological'[147] were it not that this might mislead some into thinking that some actual entity has been *added* to the more complex system. There is no justification for making such assertions (as, for example, in the discredited vitalist postulate). In such instances, there is a *prima facie* case that the concepts and referential terms of the theories deployed in relation to the more complex levels actually refer to new realities distinctively emerging at those levels of complexity. One example we have already seen in the case of DNA, in conjunction with its co-evolved cytoplasm, when there emerges a genuine capacity to convey information not present in individual nucleotides. Others occur at many different levels in Figure 1, usually known best to the practioners of the corresponding fields of study.

Figure 1

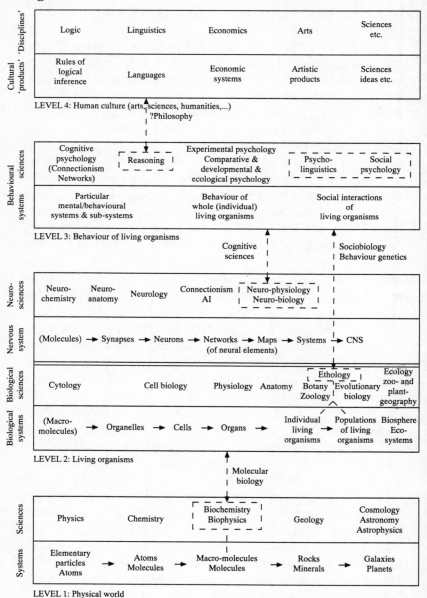

Figure 1

Legend to Figure 1

A 'hierarchy of disciplines' (an elaboration of Figure 8.1 of Bechtel and Abrahamsen[145]. 'Levels' correspond to foci of interest and so of analysis (see text). Level 4 is meant to give only an indication of the content of human culture (cf. Popper's 'World 3').

Solid horizontal arrows represent part-to-whole hierarchies of structural and/or functional organization. (N.B. Molecules and macro-molecules in level 1 are the lowest 'parts' of the 'wholes' in level 2).

Dashed boxes represent sub-disciplines in particular levels that can be coordinated with studies at the next higher level (the connections are indicated by vertical, dashed, double-headed arrows).

In each of the levels 1–3, examples are given of the *systems* studied which can be classified as being within these levels and also of their corresponding scientific disciplines.

Level 2 elaborates additionally the part-whole hierarchy of levels of organization in the nervous system (after Fig. 1 of Churchland and Sejnowski).

In level 2, the science of genetics has relevance to the whole range of the part-whole hierarchy of living systems and so, if included, would have to be written so as to extend across its entire width.

CNS = central nervous system.

Thus we have here a contemporary version of Sir Thomas Browne's vertical Scale of Nature, except it now has a fascinating convergence with his horizontal one of history, at least insofar as it concerns the non-human. For the kind of hierarchy of increasing complexities which constitutes the world as it now is corresponding very closely to its past development in time in cosmic and terrestrial biological evolution, in which the more complex can only emerge from the less so. Whether or not human history has the directional character in which he believed is, of course, still one of the religious affirmations at issue.

Critical realism, a contemporary 'scale' of being and becoming and the reality of the personal

The foregoing interpretations of the relations between the sciences and the realities of the natural world presuppose that the scientific studies denoted in Figure 1 (and others not included here), whether or not humanity is their field of interest, actually can refer in their concepts and the terms of their theories to what is distinctively real in that upon which they focus. That is, these scientific studies aim, at least, to depict reality and can do so through the use of revisable metaphors and models deployed within the context of a continuous linguistic community. This stance, often now called that of 'critical realism' commends itself to me as the appropriate description of both the scientific and theological enterprises, though the latter would take a separate justification. Suffice it that it certainly seems to be the working philosophy of most practising scientists and most practising religious believers. In their intellectual accounts, both, for me, involved inference to the best explanation based on the normal criteria of reasonableness (fit with the data, internal coherence, comprehensiveness, fruitfulness and general cogency).

Such considerations, it gradually dawned on me, now allow us to infer from the new map of knowledge a new 'scale' (to use Sir Thomas' word) of being and becoming. Science has shown that the natural world is a hierarchy of levels of complexity, each operating at its own level, and each requiring its own methods of inquiry and developing its own conceptual framework, in which at least some of the terms can refer to new non-reducible realities distinctive of the level in question. In a nutshell, atoms and molecules are not more real than cells, or living organisms, or ecosystems. Moreover there are social and personal realities too. For this recognition of the possibility of the emergence of new realities in the natural world, as one moves up Figure 1, gives a recognizable location within the map of knowledge for the emergence of the distinctively human, all that is signalled by the use of the word 'person'. The language of personal experience, especially that of personal relations, thereby acquires a new legitimacy as referring to realities which could be emergent in humanity and which are not prematurely to be reduced to the concepts applicable to the constituents of the evolved human body. They must be accorded a *prima facie* status of referring to realities until they have unequivocally been shown to be reducible totally to the sciences of the lower levels. And this has not happened. For it is notable that even philosophers who take a non-dualist view of the mind/body problem often recognize the inherent non-reducibility of mentalistic language to that of the brain and cognitive sciences. The total, complex brain states of consciousness can thus still be regarded as realities known from within and expressed *faute de mieux* in the ordinary language of personal experiences and relations – and not only ordinary language. For is it not time that those of us who have been educated predominantly in the sciences recognize frankly, indeed gratefully, that the most accurate and sensitive means for expressing states of human consciousness and personal relations are to be found not in the language of the sciences – especially not in those of artificial intelligence or of connectionism – but in those of the arts (verbal, musical, physical and visual) and even of religion? In this perspective, personhood is an emergent reality in biological evolution and history and any account of personal life has a distinctive core which is not reducible to the concepts and referential terms of the theories of the sciences that focus upon the less complex levels of human beings (all those in Levels 1–3 of Figure 1) – although, of course, it depends on the proper operation of processes at those levels.

The legitimacy of theology and the questions to which it responds

These reflections led me to perceive how theology (talk about God: theo-logy) might be given at least a provisional justification by locating it on this map of knowledge. God, we have postulated, transcends while giving existence to all-that-is, as Source of all being and becoming. God cannot then be in any sense an 'emergent' reality, for God is the ultimate Reality that relates to all that is created, which is everything other than Godself. Hence at the topmost limit of the scale of complex relations in any schema, one cannot but place the relation of God to the world and to human persons in the world (possessing as they do the most complex piece of matter in that world, the human brain). This leads us to expect, from the map we have been outlining, that the language needed to articulate these relationships should be distinctive and *sui generis*, God and the world both being real on this understanding. Thus theology can find a legitimate location on such a map and its concepts and the terms in its theories (usually called 'doctrines') can refer to realities and are not prematurely to be reduced to those of, say, physiology, anthropology or sociology. It will be a matter of investigation to see how far that is possible at all. But there is moreover a particular reason why we can expect that such reduction of theology will never be totally exhaustive. For its 'object', its focus of interest, is 'God' that which, the One Who, by definition, is other than all-that-is and greater than we can conceive. Therefore this focus of study, God, is not *ex hypothesi* describable by anything in the world and reference to God can be only through inherently inadequate analogy, in metaphor and model.

The map of knowledge and the scale of being and becoming which I have been sketching also reinforces another question with theological import which relentlessly impressed itself upon me as a scientist. It was: 'What kind of explanation of the existence of this universe is plausible and most consistent with all the data, when we take account of the now well-established fact that the original quantum fluctuation[148] has by the operation of its own inherent processes, as unravelled by the sciences, given rise to the emergence of free, self-conscious persons, capable of thought, prayer, creativity and of adherence of (and repudiation of) values of truth, beauty and goodness?'

It seemed, and still seems, to me that the cutting edge of this question has been immeasurably sharpened by the evolutionary vista that the sciences of the last century and a half have unveiled to us. It demands, more insistently than ever was possible in the days of the fallible Argument from Design, to be most coherently responded to by postulating that the One, rational Source of Being and Becoming that we call 'God' is also working out what we can only call a 'purpose,' utilising the most potent language we can command, that which also pertains to where the process has so far been going – namely, the language of the personal. So we have to insist that God is at *least* personal; that personal language, necessarily analogical and metaphorical as it is, is the least misleading way of referring to this unique and ultimate Reality; that God may then said to be 'rational' and 'purposive' in the eliciting of persons through the processes of the created world which the sciences discover.

At once a paradox arises. We have postulated that this 'God' transcends all-that-is in giving it being and becoming; yet, by creating through its very processes, is also immanent in all-that-is. This paradox is implicit in many of the major religious traditions who cope with it in various ways. The Christian faith embraces the paradox and adds a *tertium quid*, God as *Logos*, the self-expressive outreach of God in the very forms of the created order, as the transcendence of the Immanent and the immanence of the Transcendent. A provisional model of this last, it always seemed to me, is the kind of transcendence-in-immanence/immanence-in-transcendence which we humans experience in the relation of our self-conscious intentions and purposes to the bodies which implement them and which are also our own selves in action. So Christians have traditionally affirmed three modalities of the way in which the one God relates to the world — whether or not they constitute the ultimate mystery of God's own Being and Becoming continues to be the concern of, to me, an obscure but obviously profound debate which, frankly, I find I cannot avoid suspecting of being a fruitless attempt to scale the walls of the citadel of the ultimately Ineffable.

Science and the possibility of God interacting and communicating with the world

I have spoken of God's relation to the world in general terms, but how are we to conceive of God's action in or, as many contributors to the discussion prefer to put it, God's interaction with the world? This is a crucial question for our times and especially challenges the religion of a scientist who has to take seriously the every-expanding ability of the sciences to unravel the causal nexus of the first three levels in Figure 1. For the option of conceiving God as a kind of *deus ex machina* who disrupts the very regularities Godself has created hardly seems worthy of the purposive, supra-rational Creator God who gives existence to this subtly rational and beautiful articulated world, whose existence and character must form the very basis for a scientist (*qua scientist*) of believing in the existence of such a creative God in the first place. In what follows I can but offer my own perspective in my personal *religio philosophi naturalis*.

The monotheistic religions all recongnize that God is the source of the existence of the world (all-that-is other than God) and continues, in our (created) time, to give it existence as each moment succeeds another. But how can we regard God as inter-

Figure 2

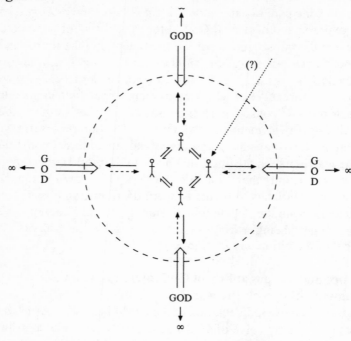

GOD   is represented by the whole surface of the page, imagined to extend to infinity (∞) in all directions

(·)   the WORLD, all-that-is: created and other than God and including -

Ⴕ   HUMANITY

⟹   God's interaction with and influence on the world and its events - both general and particular

---- ▸   effects of the non-human world on humanity

——▸   human agency in the non-human world

⇌   personal interactions, both individual and social, between human beings

·········▸   *direct* communication from God to humanity?

Diagram representing spatially the interaction between God and the world, including humanity.

acting with the world in such a way as actually to make a difference to events and so to patterns of events? The situation is depicted in Figure 2 which is an attempt to give a representation, rather like a Venn diagram, both of the world being 'in God', that God is immanent in the world and present to it all; and of God being more than the world, of God transcending the world. There is more to God than the world which is of a different kind of existent altogether than God (so Figure 2 is pan-*en*-theistic in intention and not pantheistic). Human beings are emergent within nature and so lie fully within the circle denoting the 'world'. Within that circle all is 'natural,' that is, fundamentally intelligible to the disciplines of the natural and human sciences, taking account of their due limitations already discussed, and are therefore sub-sumable under certain rubrics of regularity, however putative (commonly called the 'laws of nature', though this term hardly seems appropriate to the human sciences and even has drawbacks in the physical sciences). The only lacunae in the nexus of causes and effects, saving that of human free will, are those at the level of quantum events, predictable only probabilistically in their outcomes; and the macroscopic, so-called 'chaotic' states of non-linear, deterministic, dynamical systems which now transpire to be extremely sensitive to initial conditions so that *we* can never know those conditions with sufficient accuracy to predict the future sequence of states over an indefinite period. Some argue that God's action in the world is best located in one or other of these lacunae, the unclosable gaps in our knowledge. Macroscopic events could then be altered by God without infringing the regularities science reports.

I am unhappy with these suggestions for various reasons. Briefly, in the case of a *divine* quantum 'intervention', there is the problem of God's knowledge of the outcome of individual quantum events if there are no hidden variables; and in this case and that of 'chaotic' systems (which anyway *are* deterministic), there is the doubt that it can scarcely be an argument for God's altering those macroscopic states that we can never, in principle, know whether or not God has acted to change them.

So, we continue to ask, how can we conceive of God's interacting to influence patterns of events in the world when all seems

subsumable under the regularities of the sciences? – a question
that persists as a thorn in the flesh of a scientist seeking a believable religion. I offer therefore a sketch of my own path through
the jungle. I have been under contribution from three areas which
have helped me to model how God might interact with the world
to change patterns of events consistently with my scientific
perceptions. They are as follows.

(1). *The existence of top-down causation, or whole-part
constraints*. In many complex systems (whose complexity can be
structural and/or functional and/or temporal), the macroscopic
state and character of the system as whole is a constraint upon,
effectively like a cause, on what happens to the units of which it
is constituted, so that these latter behave in ways other that they
would have done were they not part of that system.

(2). *The concept of information transfer*. 'Information' has
overlapping and connected meanings (as classified by John
Puddefoot): (a) counting-information in communication theory,
concerned with the probability of outcomes or cases when there
are multiple possibilities; (b) shaping-information, the process of
giving form to something (cf. Latin *informare*: to give shape to);
(c) meaning-information in the ordinary sense of knowledge.
Puddlefoot[149] points out that information (a) must inform our
brains/minds in sense (b) to convey information in sense (c). This
whole process – (a), (b) and (c) – I shall henceforth refer to as an
input, or communication, of information to our brains/
minds. Note that the process begins with (a) which is conceptu-
ally distinct from the transfer of energy with which it is invariably
linked in our observed world.

(3). *Recent interpretations of the mind-brain interaction and so of
personal agency*. The way the brain acts on the body through the
operation of the central nervous system is best conceived, according to the brain scientist Roger Sperry,[150] as an instance of such
top-down causation or whole-part constraint. The total state of the
human brain-as-a-whole, a state self-consciously describable to
ourselves only in mentalistic language, is a constraint upon, and
so causally effective, on the firing of individual neurones, or
groups of neurones, in such a way as to trigger, and actually be the
specific action intended in the consciousness that was the brain

state. This amounts to a contemporary analysis of what is involved in personal agency.[151]

These considerations, taken together, have led me[152] to envisage that a suitable model for God's interaction with the world is that of God as 'informing', influencing through an input of information (in the general sense expounded above), and so shaping and influencing, the whole state of all-that-is over all space and all times. Thereby God exerts a top-down causative constraint so that particular patterns of events at lower levels within that whole can, if God so wills, be different from what they would otherwise have been if God had not so willed; and if God had left the interplay of law and chance to continue to operate in the general processes of the world, as God's general will continuously prescribes. But in being different from what they might otherwise have been, apart from this specific intention of God, these events do not in any way deviate from any of the regularities ('laws') which pertain to their particular level in the world (1–4, Figure 1) – any more than do the constituents of systems (physical, biological, social), which exert top-down causation, or whole-part constraint, on their lower levels as in (1) above. God alone has the all-embracing comprehensive knowledge of, and presence to, all-that-is through all time and space, so such an interaction must be unique to God alone. It is analogous to personal agency, as expounded in (3) above, and also to what the biblical tradition affirms. The ultimate 'how' question in this model (and remember it is only a model) is how God can input information without an input of energy. This is unanswerable and one can only resort to saying that this is a 'direct action' of God, for *all* theories of God's interaction with the world eventually run into the problem of the 'ontological gap at the causal joint' (Austin Farrer) – the recognition that there will always be a gap in our understanding because there is an unbridgeable ontological gulf between what God is in God's own self and all created entities, that is, everything other than God (which is what *creatio ex nihilo* is about). My proposal is simply one concerning the location in relation to the world of this ontological gap across which God, as it were, acts directly. The suggestion is therefore that there is one continuing act of God on the whole that can manifest itself in patterns of events which constitute meaning for those creatures, namely ourselves, who have the capacity to discern them. Thus does God communicate Godself to free self-conscious persons whose existence God has purposed and elicited through the natural, creative processes to which God continues to give existence. Thus these patterns or events can thereby constitute meanings for us which God intends to convey: we come here close to the idea of God's self-expressive Word (the *Logos*) as manifest in and imprinted upon the whole created order and process.

Communication between God and humanity

The idea that patterns of events can constitute meaning for human beings and so be a means of self-communication from God to humanity is in fact a characteristically personal mode of inter-action. For when we as persons interact with each other, we do so through interpretable patterns in electromagnetic waves of light (sight), vibrations in the air (sound), molecules (taste and smell) and physical pressure (touch) – all of which are irreducibly physical as means without derogating from the subtleties of inter-personal interaction. So it is not surprising that God should use the same means of interpretable patterns of events in the natural (including human) world to communicate with us. Of course, as human beings we have to learn how to read the signals others, individually and corporately, send to us in those complex patterns in time and space we call language (written, verbal, bodily), music, art, etc. Subtle as human communication is, its means are physical, even though the content of the messages are personal and can be the most profound of which we are capable. Thus, God's signals, if they *are* there, have to be read and interpreted, no less that the writing on the wall in Belshazzar's feast. Old Sir Thomas Browne is worth recalling at this point: 'The Hand of Providence writes often by Abbreviatures, Hieroglyphics or short Characters ... which are not to be made out but by a Hint or Key from the Spirit which indited them'.[153]

Sir Thomas' remark should serve to give us pause. For

- if God is anything like what I have been depicting,

- if God has created and continues to create a world in which free persons have emerged and flourish, and
- if God is least misleadingly described as personal and implements the divine purposes by eliciting the emergence of a humanity that seeks God as its Source and Ground –

then, might not the same humanity have grounds for hoping that God's own self is perennially initiating communication to that very same humanity, alone in all creation capable of responding freely and consciously to God's signals? Surely the human search for God must therefore be matched by, indeed transcended by, God's own communication to humanity in what we can then only call 'revelation'?

Thus it is that the scientist can find him- or herself, in spite of the inherited prejudice of the tribe, having seriously to consider the content of those major religions that make claims to conserve revelations of God to humanity in the past and to continue to be channels of experience of God today. That barrier of prejudice is, of course, enormous after a century of the trumpeting of the supposed 'warfare' between 'religion' and 'science' and the alienation of the respective communities. But now that the autonomy of science from interference by religious bodies is secure, surely it is time for scientists to grow out of that period of rebellious adolescence to consider maturely the challenge of the most profound thinking about human existence to which the existence of the phenomenon of religion testifies, ever since – one might dare to say – the Neanderthals buried their dead with ritual?

We all, scientists included, have a major inquiry to undertake into the well-winnowed wisdom of the religions of the world concerning God's communication and relation to humanity – in spite of the horrific deeds done to human beings in the name of intolerant religion. For the corruption of the best is still the worst and science, too, has its corruptions: none of us can afford to be 'holier than thou.'

A scientist explores the Christian religion

I can only indicate briefly where my thinking and experience have led me in the context of the post-Christian society in which

I have lived. My own quest was influenced by the need, instilled in me by my scientific training, to ask 'Why?', to ask 'What is the evidence for?' any particular proposals or positions in religion, as in science, and not to accept uncritically any claimed authorities, for such assertions are almost invariably circular in the validation of their presumed authority.

If, as I have argued, it is reasonable to expect that God communicates through patterns of events in the world, the claim that the history of the ancient people of Israel is such a revelation is *prima facie* worthy of investigation. I have indeed found[154] that the record of this revelation in their scriptures is enriching of my understanding of God, provided they are studied in the light of historical, critical scholarship and with the recognition that there is much dross amongst the gold – inevitably since those scriptures are a selected library of a culture extending over a thousand years.

The same considerations concerning the possibility of God's self-communication also render it possible that a human being might emerge who so freely responds to God that he/she is able to be 'informed,' and thus shaped, by God so as to be a unique vehicle for God's self-expression in the world; and so to be able both to convey God's own meanings for human existence to us all and to be a window into the divine life itself. In Jesus of Nazareth, I believe we have grounds for saying that this has happened within the matrix of the revelation of God through the ancient people of Israel – that is, that Jesus was the God-informed person *par excellence*, and so identifiable as a self-expression of God in human form. As traditionally affirmed, he was the Word, *Logos*, of God 'made [human] flesh'. I regard this capacity that he demonstrated to be, in principle, a possibility for all humanity in an inclusive understanding of what is technically known as the Incarnation. But I also affirm it actually occurred in and to him and that we have evidence that his life was taken up into that of God's own self. In his human life of suffering, self-sacrificial love for his fellow human beings we have then a revelation of both what humanity is intended to be and become in the purposes of God, and what God perennially is. Thus he came to be called the 'Christ,' the Anointed One to fulfil this mission.

During that life, he initiated a new human community whose

very *raison d'être* was and is the instantiation of a new possibility for human life – that of openness to God in self-offering love. I also think that, amongst much else, Jesus also initiated a repeating pattern of events in which that community might realize specifically the personal presence of God that had been manifest in him. I refer to the sacraments of the church in which created matter – natural and/or 'the work of human hands' (bread, wine, oil, water) – is incorporated into an authorized act of the community Jesus initiated in such a way that God can be present effectively and cognitively, as surely as we encounter human persons through patterns of physical signs, as we have seen. This sacramental character of at least the Christian religion has been central to me in my own particular pilgrimage, for the sacraments are in explicit and repeatedly manifest sign of what the scientist perceives as going on in cosmic and biological evolution – namely, the very stuff of the world acquiring spiritual capacities in becoming the vehicle of personhood. I have indicated how the sacraments fit into my account of God's general relation to the world and with respect to the unnecessarily, controversial interpretations of the meaning of, in particular, the Eucharist or Holy Communion, I prefer the affirmative reticence of Queen Elizabeth the First:

> 'Twas God the word that spake it,
> He took the Bread and brake it;
> And what the world did make it;
> That I believe, and take it.[155]

Humility before God and nature

This quotation brings us full circle to that culture with which I began this sketch of how a twentieth-century scientist can begin to take seriously the revelation of God in certain strands in human history. It was and is no intention of mine to foreclose on the possibility that God has spoken at 'sundry times and in diverse manners'[156] to other people of other cultures. But science, as we know it, is now the independent offspring of a Christian culture, so it is not surprising that this scientist, at least, should find his spiritual home in that tradition, however critically appropriated.

Once one had decided that God *is*, one has taken the first step on a long journey that will last a lifetime, indeed into eternity, and one will need all the sources of spiritual discipline that the experience and wisdom of the community of followers of this Way can provide (prayer, worship, meditation, the sacraments ...). But not that community alone, for being a lover as well as a student of nature, one of my greatest joys is walking the English countryside – as its best a co-creation of God and humanity – and in the Scottish mountains – wild and untouched, as God has been making them. Then, occasionally, with Wordsworth at Tintern Abbey on the Wye:

> '... I have felt
> A presence that disturbs me with joy
> Of elevated thoughts; a sense sublime
> Of something far more deeply interfused,
> Whose dwelling is the light of setting suns,
> And the round ocean and the living air,
> And the blue sky, and in the mind of man.'[157]

In all of these spiritual experiences of a natural scientist, my *religio philosophi naturalis*, there is one pre-condition that all explorers into realities, natural and divine, must fulfil. It was the attitude expressed in a prayer of that devout man with whom I began, Sir Thomas Browne:

> 'Teach my endeavours so thy workes to read,
> That learning them, in thee I may proceed.' (p. 76)

This need for humility, has never been better expressed than by that arch-hammer of ecclesiastics and Darwin's 'bull-dog,' Thomas H. Huxley, who wrote in a letter to Charles Kingsley, the author and Evangelical clergyman,

> 'Science seems to me to teach in the highest and strongest manner the great truth which is embodied in the Christian conception of entire surrender to the will of God. Sit down before fact as a little child, be prepared to give up every

preconceived notion, follow humbly wherever and to whatever abysses Nature leads, or you shall learn nothing. I have
only begun to learn content and peace of mind since I
resolved at all risks to do this.'[158]

END NOTES

1. *An Introduction to the Physical Chemistry of Biological Organization* (Clarendon Press, Oxford, 1983; paperback, 1989).
2. *Il Paradiso*, Canto XXXIII, ll. 142–5 (Trans. Barbara Reynolds, Penguin Books, London, 1962).
3. Thomas Sprat, *The History of the Royal Society of London for the Improving of Natural Knowledge* (London, 1702, 2nd end.), pp. 370–2.
4. *Creation and the World of Science* (Clarendon Press, Oxford, 1979).
5. *Intimations of Reality: Critical Realism in Science and Religion* (University of Notre Dame Press, Notre Dame, Indiana, 1984).
6. In a publication exploring widely disparate conceptions of the nature of the human 'person' (*Persons and Personality*, eds. Arthur Peacocke and Grant Gillett, Blackwells, Oxford, 1987); and interdisciplinary reports on *Values, Conflict and the Environment* (to be published in 1996 in book form by Avebury, Aldershot, England, U.K.); on *Quality of Life and the Practice of Medicine* (obtainable from the Ian Ramsey Centre, Theology Faculty Centre, 41 St Giles, Oxford OX1 3LW, England, U.K.); and on *Medicine and Moral Reasoning*, eds. K. W. M. Fulford, G. Gillett, J. Martin Soskice, (Cambridge University Press, Cambridge, 1994).
7. The Ian Ramsey Centre continued until 1994 under the direction of Caroline Miles, who obtained funds to develop a course in ethics, communication skills and the law for clinical medical students. In 1995 I was re-appointed Director to administer a significant grant from the Templeton Foundation for the Centre to organise workshops in 1996 and beyond for those giving courses in science and religion.
8. The proceedings are published as *Evolution and Creation: A European Perspective*, eds. S. Andersen and A. Peacocke (Aarhus University Press, 1987).
9. The first printed reference to this proposal, not at the time at all well formulated, is in an article of mine, entitled 'The Church in an Age of Science' in the *Church Times* of 26th January, 1962.
10. See chapter 26 below for a further exposition of this.
11. *Christian Believing: the nature of the Christian faith and its expression in Holy Scripture and creeds*, a report by the Doctrine Commission of the Church of England (SPCK, London, 1976).
12. Rom. 8, v.19 (NSRV).
13. Rom. 8, vv.19–21 (NSRV).
14. Dorothy Sayers, 'The greater images' in The Divine Comedy, vol. I. (Penguin Books, Harmondsworth, 1949), p. 68.
15. John Donne, *An Anatomie of the World: The First Anniversary*.
16. *Acts* 17, v.28 (AV).
17. Isa. 40, vv.26, 28 (AV).
18. I am thinking here of those macroscopic phenomena which result from the amplification of inherently indeterministirc quantum events occurring at the micro level. Some patterns of macroscopic events are also unpredictable because of 'chaotic' dynamics, but these are not inherently indeterministic, only very sensitive to initial conditions.

215

19. Quoted by Kathleen Raine in *William Blake* (Thames and Hudson, London, 1970), pp. 186–7.
20. Thomas Traherne, *Centuries*, 3,3.
21. Job 38 v.6,7 (AV).
22. From T. S. Eliot, *The Four Quartets*: The Dry Salvages.
23. Quoted by Karl Popper in his 'intellectual autobiography', *Unended Quest*, (Collins, London, 1976), p. 59 [his translation; see p. 206, n. 59 for details].
24. Eph. 5, v.19 (NRSV).
25. Luke 13, v.4 (REB).
26. Eccl. 9 v.11 (REB).
27. D. J. Bartholomew, *God of Chance* (SCM Press, London, 1984), p. 82.
28. John Donne, *Holy Sonnets*, (2) v.
29. Julian of Norwich, *Revelations of Divine Love*, 68.
30. Genesis 3 v.5 (NSRV).
31. F. J. A. Hort, *The Way, the Truth and the Life* (Macmillan, Cambridge and London, 1893), p. 213.
32. George Herbert, *Providence*.
33. Rom. 1, v.19–20 (REB).
34. Exod. 3.
35. Ps. 47, v.10.
36. Amos 2, v.6 (REB).
37. Amos 5, v.24 (REB).
38. R. Alter and F. Kermonde, eds., *The Literary Guide to the Bible* (Collins, London, 1987), p. 34.
39. Matt. 5 v.17 (REB).
40. Cf., Ps .119 v.92.
41. John 1, v.14 (AV).
42. 1. Cor. 1, v.24 (REB).
43. Col. 2, v.3 (REB).
44. Karl Jaspers, *The Origin and Goal of History* (Routledge and Kegan Paul, London, 1953), p.2.
45. *Times*, 6 June 1991.
46. J. Macquarrie, *Jesus Christ in Modern Thought* (SCM Press, London, 1990), pp. 51–2.
47. Ibid., p. 52–3, quoting E. P. Saunders.
48. J. A. T. Robinson, *The Human Face of God* (SCM Press, London, 1973), p. 179.
49. Jer. 31, v.31 (REB).
50. 2 Cor. 5, v.19 (AV).
51. P. Fiddes, *The creative suffering of God* (Clarendon Press, Oxford, 1988), p. 31.
52. Gal. 4, v.19 (AV).
53. Mark 10, v.39 (REB).
54. 2 Cor. 5, v.17 (REB).
55. A. M. Ramsey, *The Resurrection of Christ* (Fontana edition, 1961), p. 9.
56. 1. Cor. 15, v.3 (REB).
57. Paul in Rom. 1.3f. and the use of Psalm 2, v.7 ('You are my son ... this day I become your father'), especially in Acts 13, v.33.
58. 1. Cor. 15, v.8 (REB).
59. Q.v., chapter 13.
60. Heb. 1, v.2 (NEB).
61. Rom. 8, v.29,30 (REB).
62. Luke 24, v.51 (NRSV).
63. Origen, *de Orat.* 23.1.
64. Gal. 4, v.19 (NRSV).
65. Eph. 4, v.13 (NRSV).
66. W. Temple, *Fellowship with God* (1920), p.108.

67. Heb. 2, v.10 (NRSV).
68. 1. Cor. 2, v.11 (REB).
69. G. Steiner, *Real Presences* (Faber and Faber, London and Boston, 1989) pp. 226–7.
70. John 14, v.16; 16, v.15 (NRSV).
71. Rom. 8, vv.14–17 (NRSV).
72. Deut. 6, v.4 (RSV).
73. 1 John 4, v.8.
74. Rom. 8, v.26 (NRSV).
75. *We Believe in God*, Report of the Doctrine Commission of the Church of England (Church House Publishing, London, 1987), p. 108. I am deeply indebted to this section of this Report for much of what follows.
76. 1. Cor. 12, v.3 (NRSV).
77. Gal. 2, v.20 (NRSV).
78. John 14, v.12 (all English versions).
79. Rom. 8, v.17: '… joint heirs with Christ – if, in fact, we suffer with him so that we may be glorified with him' (NSRV).
80. F. D. Maurice, *Theological Essays*, 1905, XVI, p. 354.
81. Thomas Chalmers, *The Power and Wisdom of God*, 1st Bridgewater Treatise, (1832) (3rd edit., William Pickering, London), vol. II, pp. 129–130.
82. Deut. 11, vv.18–9 (AV).
83. Micah 6, v.8 (AV).
84. Phil. 3, vv.12–4 (REB).
85. Mark 13, vv.35,37 (NRSV).
86. Keith Ward, *The Turn of the Tide* (BBC Publications, London, 1986).
87. 2 Cor. 11. vv.25–7 (RSV).
88. Phil. 3, vv.5–8 (RSV).
89. Rom. 7, vv.15,18,19–25 (RSV).
90. !. Cor. 1, vv.13,29–30 (RSV).
91. Gal. 3, v.28 (RSV).
92. Paul Fiddes, *The Creative Suffering of God*, (Clarendon Press, Oxford, 1988), p.3.
93. Rev. 13, v.8 (AV).
94. *Op.cit.*, p. 31.
95. E. Weisel, *Night* (Penguin Books, Harmondsworth, 1981), pp. 76–7.
96. A. N. Whitehead, *Process and Reality* (Cambridge University Press, 1929), p. 497.
97. Rom. 8, vv.16–18, 38–9 (REB).
98. C. E. Trinkhaus, *In Our Image and Likeness: Humanity and Divinity in Italian Humanist Thought* (Constable, London, 1970), p. 248.
99. See section II, chaps. 4 and 5, above.
100. Kathleen Raine, *William Blake* (Thames and Hudson, London, 1970), pp. 186–7.
101. Teilhard de Chardin, *Le Milieu Divin* (Fontana Books, London, 1964), pp. 64ff.
102. J. Moltmann, 'Hope and the biomedical future of man', *Hope and the Future of Man*, ed. E. H. Cousins (Fortress Press, Philadelphia, and Garnstone Press, London, 1972), p. 90.
103. Proverbs 29, v.18 (AV).
104. Leo Tolstoy, *The Death of Ivan Ilyach and other Stories*, (World's Classics, Oxford University Press, London, 1971, transl. L. & A. Maude), pp. 44–45.
105. Alexander Pope, *An Essay on Man*, Epistle ii, 1.28.
106. 2 Cor. 5, vv.18–20 (RSV).
107. Mark 15, v.34 (REB).
108. John Donne, 'Sermon preached at St Paul's upon Christmas Day in the Evening', 1624, in *LXXX Sermons*, 1640.
109. In the University Church, Oxford, on 14th June, 1964, published as 'A New Prospect in Theological Studies', in *Theology*, LXVII, No. 34 (1964), pp. 527–533.

110. The Ian Ramsey Centre, Oxford, began its work on January 1st, 1985. More recently, in 1996, it has been engaged in organising workshops on the relation of science and religion with the support of the John Templeton Foundation. See also chapter 1, Section 1, 'From DNA to Dean' and n.7.
111. Matt. 13, v.52 (NEB).
112. Clifford Longley in the *Times* of February 15th, 1988.
113. H. Butterfield, *The Origins of Modern Science* (Bell, London, 1968) p.vii.
114. Quoted by J. H. Brooke, *Science and Religion: some historical perspectives* (Cambridge University Press, Cambridge, 1991), p. 1.
115. *Independent*, 5th March, 1992.
116. Ernan MacMullin, 'The case for scientific realism', in *Scientific Realism*, ed. J. Leplin (University of California Press, Berkeley, 1984), p. 30.
117. See *inter alia* Janet Martin Soskice, *Metaphor and Religious Language* (Clarendon Press, Oxford, 1984), Chap. 7; and Sallie MacFague, *Models of God* (SCM Press, London, 1987).
118. See, for example, my *Theology for a Scientific Age* (*TSA*, 2nd, enlarged edit., SCM Press, London, and Fortress Press, Minneaplis, 1993), Introduction.
119. B. G. Mitchell, *The Justification of Religious Belief* (Macmillan, London, 1973); M. Banner, *The Justification of Science and the Rationality of Religious Belief* (Clarendon Press, Oxford, 1990).
120. *Ibid.*
121. I cannot trace the reference.
122. Hans Küng in an unpublished lecture, 'Paradigm change in theology', given at the University of Chicago in 1981 and now published in a different form in *Paradigm Change in Theology*, eds. Hans Küng and David Tracy (T. & T. Clark, Edinburgh, 1989, pp. 3–33.
123. But this response is not undisputed, for mathematical physicists take very seriously – even reifying – their models of a 4-dimensional, 'block' universe in which the future just *is* there already, so to speak. (See the recent discussion between C. J. Isham and J. C. Polkinghorne of the issues involved in this in 'The Debate over the Block Universe', as *Quantum Cosmology and the Laws of Nature*, eds. R. J. Russell, N. Murphy and C. J. Isham (Vatican Observatory and University of Notre Dame Press, 1993), pp. 135–144.
124. This may be understood as analogous to what is technically called an input of 'information', as distinct from energy. See the discussion in *TSA*, pp. 179; chap. 11, sections 2(a), 3(b) and 3(c); and endnote 31, pp. 416–7, discussing J. C. Puddefoot's analysis of the meaning of this term (n. 149, below. See also pp. 206ff in this present volume).
125. Rom. 6, v.23 (REB).
126. John A. T. Robinson, *The Human Face of God* (SCM Press, London, 1973), p. 68 and n.3.
127. For a fuller expostition see *TSA*, chap. 13, section 3(d).
128. Q.v., *TSA*, chap. 13, section 3(e).
129. Raymond Brown, *Birth of the Messiah*, p. 527, emphasis in his text.
130. J. Macquarrie, *Jesus Christ*, pp. 392, 393.
131. Gregory of Nazianzus, Ep.101 – 380/1 in Bettenson, *Documents of the Christian Church*, p. 64 (OUP, London, 1956 repr.).
132. This does not, of course, derogate at all from St Mary's unique position in Christian devotion and affection as the mother of Our Lord, who must have been the primary influence on his maturation and one of the earliest witnesses to his true vocation and role – and in a very real sense, the Mother of the Church.
133. C. F. Evans, article on 'Resurrection' in *A New Dictionary of Christian Theology*, eds. A. Richardson and J. Bowden (SCM Press, London, 1983), p. 503.
134. For a fuller treatment, see *TSA*, pp. 319 ff.
135. The virtue of being agnostic about the relation between the 'empty tomb' and the

risen Christ here becomes apparent. For, within a relatively short time after our own biological death, our bodies will lose their identity as their atomic and molecular constituents begin to disperse through the earth and its atmosphere, often becoming part of other human beings. (See the discussion in *TSA*, pp. 279–288).

136. Irenaeus, *Adv. Haer.*, v., praef.

137. P. 75 in 'Sir Thomas Browne: The Major Works', edited by C. A. Patrides (Penguin Books, London, 1977).

138. All quotations from the *Religio Medici* and other works are cited, with page numbers, from the edition of C. A. Patrides, see n. 137.

139. Here, and elsewhere in the first part of this paper, quotations not from the *Religio Medici* itself are from the Introduction, to which I am much indebted, by C. A. Patrides to his edition of that work (see n.138). The references are to page numbers in that publication.

140. I am unable to speak first hand of any other, though what I have to say will, I hope be relevant to others forms of theism.

141. In A. Einstein, *Out of My Later Years* (repr. Greenwood Press, Westport, Conn., 1970), p. 61.

142. 'From DNA to Dean', chapter 1.

143. This term need not (*should* not) be taken to imply the operation of any influences, either external in the form of an 'entelechy' or 'life force' or internal in the sense of a 'top-down' causative influences. It is, in my usage, a purely descriptive term for the observe phenomenon of the appearance of new capabilities, functions, etc., at greater levels of complexity.

144. Francis H. C. Crick, *Of Molecules and Man* (Univ. of Washington Press, Seattle, 1966), p. 10.

145. This Figure, as well as that of Figure 2, is reproduced from *TSA*, Figure 3, p. 217. It is an elaboration of Figure 8.1 of W. Bechtel and A. Abrahamsen in *Connectionism and the Mind* (Blackwell, Oxford and Cambridge, Mass., 1991).

146. W. C. Wimsatt, 'Robustness, reliability and multiple-determination in science', in *Knowing and validating in the social sciences*: a tribute to Donald Campbell, ed. M. Brewer and B. Collins (Jossey-Bass, San Francisco, 1981).

147. This emergence of new kinds of realities is distinct in what could be called 'epistemological emergence' when the concepts and theories are not logically reducible to those pertaining to the constituents of the system. A related concept is that of 'ontological reduction' which is not usually in dispute when it is taken to refer to the fact that the complex wholes are actually made up of units which, in isolation, have their own distinctive properties – e.g., all living organisms are, in this sense, ontologically reducible to atoms and molecules and to even more 'fundamental particles'.

148. Or whatever it was on our time scale which, some 10 billion years ago, initiated the expansion of our universe.

149. John C. Puddefoot, 'Information and Creation' in *The Science and Theology of Information*, eds. C. Wassermann, R. Kirby and B. Rordorff, Proc. 3rd European Conference on Science and Theology (Editions Labor et Fides, Geneva, 1992), p. 15.

150. E.g., in his *Science and Moral Priority* (Blackwell, Oxford, 1983), ch. 6, and subsequent writings.

151. Dennis Bielfeldt, in 'God, Physicalism, and Supervenience', has recently (CTNS Bulletin, vol. 15, no. 3, Summer, 1995) argued that the concept of 'supervenience' borrowed from J. Kim's philosophy of mind-brain relations (in *Supervenience and Mind*, Cambridge University Press, Cambridge, 1993) can be effectively deployed to understand divine action within a physicalist worldview, thereby warranting the notion of God's immanent action in the world. I find the fuller working out of this idea interesting in view of my earlier espousal of this term (in *Creation and the World of Science*, Clarendon Press, Oxford, 1979, pp. 128–137, where I referred to

D. Davidson's use of this notion in connection with the mind-body problem), when utilising the model of human agency for explicating God's interaction with the world.

152. John Polkinghorne has also used the notions of input information and the idea of topdown causation from God into the world in his account, which has some differences in balance and emphasis from my own, of God's interaction with the world (J. Polkinghorne, *Science and Providence*, London, 1989), *passim.*

153. From 'Christian Morals' in 'Sir Thomas Browne: the major works', ed. C. A. Patrides (Penguin Books, London, 1977), p. 428.

154. See chapter 9, above.

155. Her answer on being asked her opinion of Christ's presence in the sacrament of the Eucharist (S. Clarke, *Marrow of Ecclesiastical History*, pt. ii, Life of Queen Elizabeth, ed. 1675).

156. *Hebrews* 1, v.1.

157. 'Lines composed a few miles above Tintern Abbey' (1798), lines 93–99, e.g. in *The Literature of England* (Chicago: Scott, Foresman and Co., 1953), p. 664.

158. See Leonard Huxley, *Life and letters of T. H. Huxley*, vol. 1 (Appleton, New York, 1913), p. 235.

INDEX

221